国际航标协会 1067指南

IALA 1067 Guideline

交通运输部南海航海保障中心 译

·广州·

版权所有　翻印必究

图书在版编目（CIP）数据

国际航标协会1067指南：英、汉／交通运输部南海航海保障中心译．—广州：中山大学出版社，2024.4
ISBN 978-7-306-08089-9

Ⅰ．①国…　Ⅱ．①交…　Ⅲ．①航标—电力系统—指南—英、汉　Ⅳ．①U644.4-62

中国国家版本馆CIP数据核字（2024）第087659号

GUOJI HANGBIAO XIEHUI 1067 ZHINAN

出 版 人：王天琪
策划编辑：张　蕊
责任编辑：张　蕊
封面设计：曾　婷
责任校对：麦颖晖
责任技编：靳晓虹
出版发行：中山大学出版社
电　　话：编辑部 020-84111997，84113349，84110283，84110779，84110776
　　　　　发行部 020-84111998，84111981，84111160
地　　址：广州市新港西路135号
邮　　编：510275　　　　传　真：020-84036565
网　　址：http://www.zsup.com.cn　　E-mail:zdcbs@mail.sysu.edu.cn
印 刷 者：广州市友盛彩印有限公司
规　　格：787mm×1092mm　1/16　9印张　160千字
版次印次：2024年4月第1版　2024年4月第1次印刷
定　　价：40.00元

如发现本书因印装质量影响阅读，请与出版社发行部联系调换

本书编译委员会

主　任	李宏印		
副主任	洪四雄		
委　员	李文华	王　平	李　伟
	赖擎青	杨　毅	姚国豪
	覃学宁	李光生	钟　辉
翻　译	杨清玲	童扬武	陈得新
	苏炳海	何文东	黄庆夫
	张　杨		
审　校	罗子汶	杨　毅	刘　锋
	陈佳丽	余锦超	邬　金
	杨　俊		

前　言

国际航标协会（The International Association of Marine Aids to Navigation and Lighthouse Authorities，IALA）是一个非营利的、非政府间的国际组织，成立于1957年，为来自世界各地区的航标管理当局、生产商和咨询机构提供一个平台，共同致力于协调全球范围内航标系统的标准，促进船舶安全、有效地航行，加强海上环境保护。

作为组织的责任之一，IALA为其成员提供标准、建议、指南及手册，促进世界范围内海上助航系统的统一和助航设备的不断改进。

《国际航标协会1067指南》作为IALA指南之一，旨在协助航标管理当局选择和设计航标的电源系统，保障航标能源供应。此次编译原则上采用原文直译，原文的词汇、释义与译稿相对应，同时为了便于理解，对部分内容进行了意译，尽量做到符合航标词汇规范和有助于航标人员的理解。

本指南总结了可用于航标的发电和储能方式及其优缺点，考虑了电能消耗和效率，优化航标能源的配备使用，帮助航标人员正确地选择和维护航标的电源系统。

因自身能力和水平有限，本书中的疏漏在所难免，敬请读者批评指正。

目　录

第 G1067-0 号
航标及相关设备的电力系统选择

1　引言

本导则旨在协助航标主管单位选择和设计航标（Aids to Navigation, AtoN）的电力系统。

本导则总结了可用于航标的发电和储能方式及其优缺点。

本导则也提出了关于生命周期管理问题的建议。

2　如何使用本导则

本导则是总体指导方针，需要结合以下导则阅读（如图 1-1 所示）：

IALA G1067-1 导则：航标的总用电负荷；

IALA G1067-2 导则：电源；

IALA G1067-3 导则：航标的电能存储。

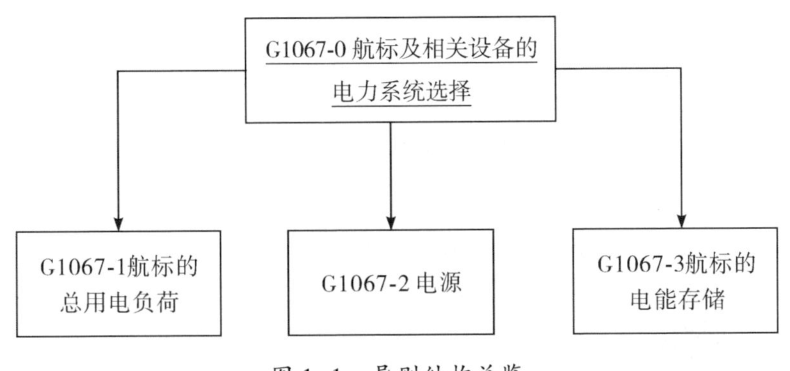

图 1-1　导则结构总览

2.1　范围

本导则注重航标电力系统工程，但也同样适用于安防系统、远程控制、监测系统和生活用电。

2.2 G1067 系列导则的应用

本导则的最佳使用流程如图 1-2 所示。

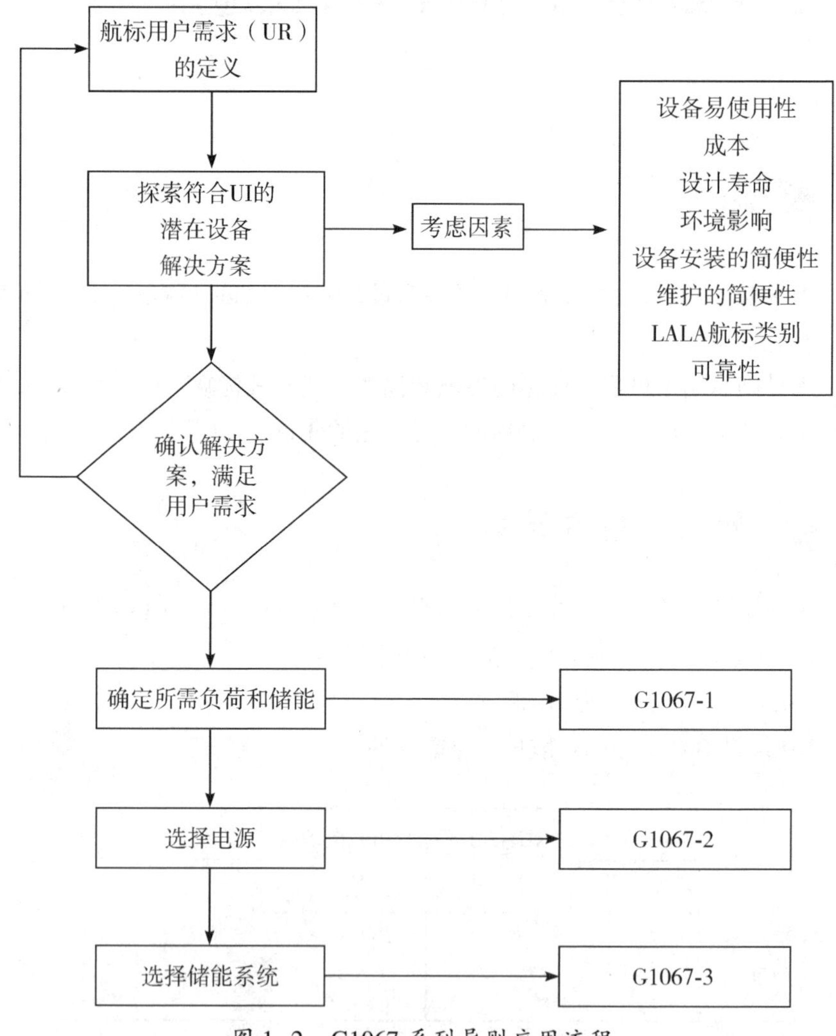

图 1-2 G1067 系列导则应用流程

3 概述

要满足航标的电力需求，不能仅考虑航标光源，而是要满足航标系统的所有设备，包括声音信号、灯光、雷康（RACON）、船舶自动识别系统（AIS）、遥测遥控、安防和生活等用电需求。生活用电量的变化很大，有人

值守的站点的用电需求将保持在一个较高的水平，而无人值守的站点的用电峰值只会在人员巡检维护时出现。

除新光源的开发外，灯塔自动化和用户需求的变化也直接影响电源的种类选择和容量配置。

然而，随着技术的发展，我们可以在不降低导助航服务标准的同时减少航标功耗。尤其是电池系统（而不是柴油发电机），可以用作航标电力的备用电源或作为可再生能源的补充。综合电力系统灯器（一体化灯器）也同样可以满足要求，从而无须外部发电和储能。

4　用户需求

用户需求对功耗有重要影响。照明距离每缩短 1 英里（约 1.6 千米），所需的发光强度就会减少一半，功耗也会因此降低。视觉和音响航标的功能需求正在发生变化，射程需求大幅减少，因此，电量需求大大降低。

▶自动化

自动化将减少对稳定的生活用电的需求，但很可能需要控制装置来确保航标设备能在需要时运行。典型的例子是用于目视航标的日光阀、用于音响航标的雾探测器和用于柴油发电机的负载控制。

▶缺点

能耗持续降低以及由此产生的用电量需求的减少是航标设施的明显优点，但如果它被应用在以前使用过的建筑物上，则应对建筑物的问题予以充分考量和解决。在潮湿条件下，建筑物本身条件会恶化，航标设备也如此（如可能是潮湿的环境导致建筑物本身以及航标设备的损坏等）。

当主供电源电量富余时，可以在不增加备用电源容量的情况下，提供暖气或冷气进行温控，以消除环境对建筑物的负面影响。然而，使用可再生能源或混合运行系统，则可能无法为建筑物调节提供富余电量，因为这会抵消所节省的开支。

在这些情况下，需要考虑替代方案，包括：

- 改善通风；
- 将建筑维护至良好状态；
- 通过高效燃气或柴油锅炉、光伏或风力发电机进行辅助动力加热/冷却；
- 使用高效率能源，如斯特林循环发动机、燃料电池等，用于供暖及供电。

5 电力系统与储能的选择

本节确定了在为航标地点选择储能和电力系统时应考虑的因素。表 1-1 提供了选择不同地点、电力需求和环境因素的最合适的电力系统的一般指南。但是，更好的做法是合理地使用指南来确定潜在的最佳解决方案。

表 1-1 航标电力系统选择指南

能源	远程站点	不易接近	大功率 >300 Wh/day	中等功率 100~300 Wh/day	低功率 < 100 Wh/day	极端温度	无法通风	浮标	大型浮标	预期寿命（估计年数）
公用电源	+o	+	++	++	+	++	++	-	-	-
柴油发电机	+	o	+	o	-	o	o	-	-	20
光伏	++	++	-	+	++	++	-	++	++	20
水平轴风力发电机	++	-	+	++	++	o	-	o	+	1~15
垂直轴风力发电机	++	-	+	++	++	++	-	+	+	10~20
燃料电池	+	o	+	++	++	o	o	-	+	5~10
波浪发电	-	-	-	+	++	o	-	+	o	3~10
混合	++	++	+	++	+	o	-	++	+	不适用

++ 推荐解决方案　　+o 公用电源可用时的推荐方案

+ 好的解决方案

o 不推荐　　- 不相关

5.1 电源指南

由第三方提供的可靠且容易获得的电力，可能是最经济的能源。在使用公用电源时，仅通过储能方式准备后备电源就足够了。储能设施的容量能维持人员进入现场并开展维修。表 1-2 提供了关于储能系统实际选择的信息，以及关于将动力源应用于海上航标的指南。

如果外部供电困难或无法安装，则应将太阳能、风能或其他可再生能源视为第二选择。在某些情况下，如果可再生能源不可用，则可以使用一次电池。

柴油发电机只应用于主负荷。

表 1-2　航标储能设备选择指南

储能		远程站点	维护需求	大功率 > 300 Wh/day	中等功率 100~300 Wh/day	低功率 < 100 Wh/day	极端温度	无法通风	浮标	主要浮标	备注
二次电池	铅酸	+	是	+	+	+	−	o	o	+	
	密封凝胶铅酸	++	否	+	+	+	+	−	++	+	
	AGM 铅酸 *	+	否	o	+	+	+	−	+	−	
	袖珍镍镉（NiCd）	++	是	+	+	+	+	o	o	+	取决于充电水平
	烧结镍镉（NiCd）	+	否	+	+	+	+	o	o	+	
	密封镍镉（NiCd）	++	否	+	+	+	+	−	++	+	
	镍（Ni）-金属氢化物	+	否	+	+	+	−	−	+	+	
	锂（二次）＊＊	+	否	+	+	+	−	−	+	+	
一次电池	空气去极化	o	否	−	−	+	o	−	+	o	
	碱性	o	否	−	−	+	o	++	+	o	
	锌-碳	−	否	−	−	+	−	++	+	−	
	锂（一次）	+	否	o	o	+	o	++	+	o	

++　推荐解决方案　　　o　不推荐

+　好的解决方案　　　−　无评论

＊ AGM：采用吸附式玻璃纤维棉。

＊＊ 在指定此电池类型时必须小心，因为电池的化学成分可能存在很大差异，从而有着不同程度的性能和安全要求。

5.2　冗余、容量和自主性

交付特定的航标时是否需要冗余的能源，是一个系统性决策，通常由航标重要性或类别来确定。可通过获取设备需求并进行风险分析，以确定最佳解决方案。

电力系统的自主性。无论备用电源是一次电源还是二次电源，都是基于代表性的、现场特定的工程生命周期分析确定的，同时还需要考虑所使用的电池特性。

已知影响能源使用寿命和储存设备的“规模和选择”的切须考虑因素包括但不限于：

- 电力负荷（峰值）；
- 可再生能源（如太阳、风）的可用性；
- 生命周期成本；
- 环境监管情况；
- 环境风险影响。

若需确定太阳能发电系统的“规模和选择”，请参阅“IALA G1039 导则：航标的太阳能发电系统设计”。

6 生命周期管理的考量

生命周期管理包括从最初的构想到最后的报废处理。周期对设备的设计和选择影响越来越大，并且与总体经费需求有直接联系。

6.1 起始阶段

6.1.1 把握航海用户的需求

任何航标项目都源于航海用户的需求，可能是一个模糊的想法，也可能是一个经过深思熟虑的方法。当为最终解决方案制定设计标准时，必须从发起机构处获得完整和简洁的设计要求。

6.1.2 设计选择的考量

应仔细考虑任何解决方案的“全寿命周期成本”，因为低成本的解决方案可能会带来非常高的运行成本，反之亦然。

因此，考虑航标“所有权”的实际成本总值非常重要。这种考量应包括诸如维护周期、设备更换周期和环境影响等问题。这些问题贯穿生命期间，因此，应当考虑当其使用寿命结束时再循环/处置的成本。

6.2 实施和服务阶段

在航标设备的使用期间，为保护周围环境，监测设备的性能是非常重要的，应采取适当措施限制维修活动对环境的影响。

对航标的巡检维护应适当保护历史遗迹，并应遵守现行规定。

建议在构想阶段就以尽可能延长巡检维护间隔的方式评估巡检维护的要求。

6.3 处置阶段

在设计阶段必须考虑所有设备的处置问题，以便减少对环境的影响。

处理含有害物质的设备变得越来越重要，必须重视对部件的返修/再利用，以延长设备的使用寿命。总之，设备的再循环优先于报废处理。应最低限度地报废处理不可重复使用的设备或部件。

重要的是，确保航标设备的任何处理都符合现行规定，并尽可能降低对环境的负面影响。

我们的后代可能会对以往的设备感兴趣，应该考虑将这些设备捐赠给博物馆。

7 缩略语

AIS automatic identification system（船舶自动识别系统）

A·h/d Ampere hour(s) per day（安培小时/天）

AtoN marine aid(s) to navigation（航海辅助标志，简称“航标”）

HAWG horizontal axis wind generator（水平轴风力发电机）

IALA International Association of Marine Aids to Navigation and Lighthouse Authorities（国际航标协会）

Ni nickel（镍）

NiCd nickel cadmium（镍镉）

RACON radar beacon（雷达信标，音译“雷康”）

UR user requirement（用户要求）

W·h/d Watt hour(s) per day（瓦时/天）

G1067-0 SELECTION OF POWER SYSTEMS FOR AtoN AND ASSOCIATED EQUIPMENT

1 INTRODUCTION

The purpose of this guideline is to assist authorities in the selection and design of power systems for Marine Aids to Navigation (AtoN).

This guideline contains a summary of power generation and energy storage options that are available for use with AtoN, together with their advantages and disadvantages.

Suggestions on life cycle management issues are also addressed in the document.

2 HOW TO USE THIS GUIDELINE

This document is an overarching guideline and needs to be read in conjunction with the following documents (See Figure 1-1):

IALA Guideline 1067-1: Total Electrical Loads of AtoN.

IALA Guideline 1067-2: Power Sources.

IALA Guideline 1067-3: Electrical Energy Storage for AtoN.

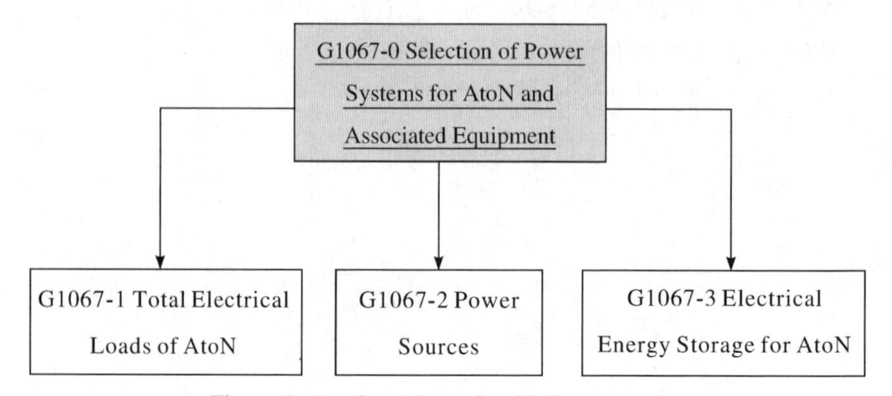

Figure 1-1 Overview of guideline structure

2.1 SCOPE

This guideline is focused on engineering of power systems for AtoN but may equally be applied to ancillary services such as security systems, remote control, monitoring and domestic loads.

2.2 APPLICATION OF THE G1067 SERIES OF GUIDELINES

Figure 1-2 shows the steps needed to make the best use of this guideline.

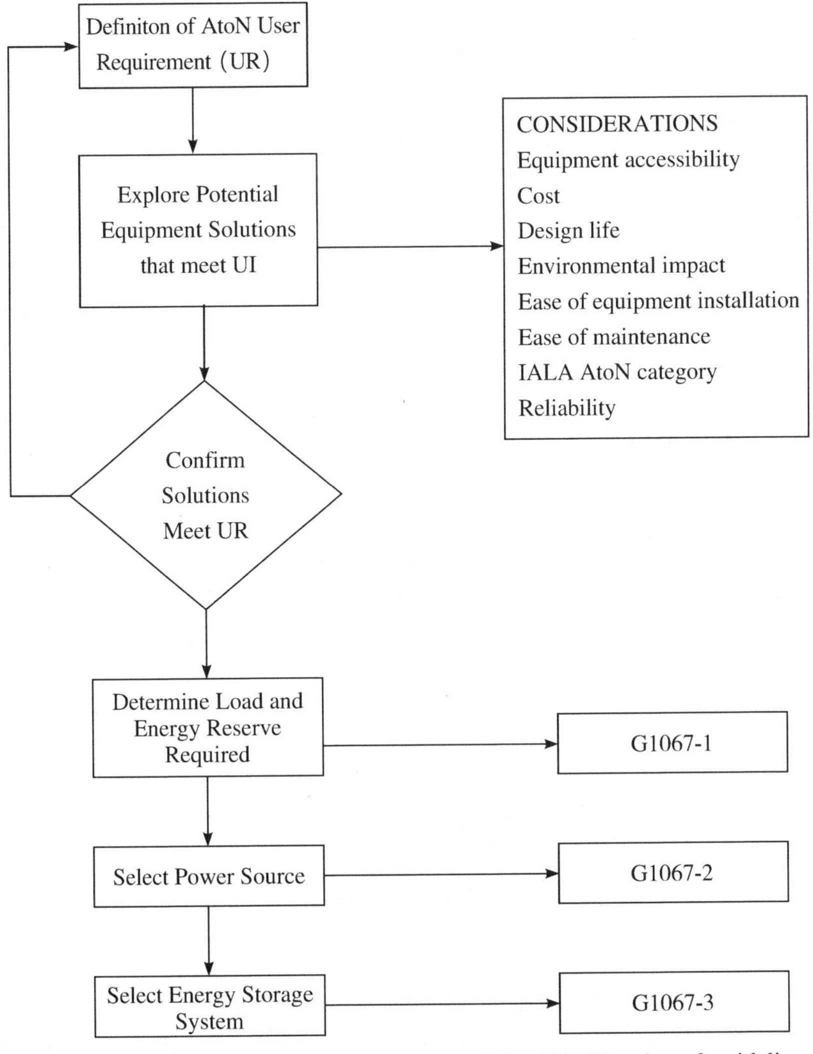

Figure 1-2 Flowchart for the application of the G1067 series of guidelines

3 GENERAL

The power requirement for AtoN cannot be based on the light source in isolation because the power system provides for the total needs of the AtoN. This may include audible signals, lights, RACONs, AIS, remote control and monitoring facilities, security and domestic loads. Domestic loads can vary substantially—demand on manned stations will be at a constant high level, while the demand on unmanned stations would only occur during maintenance visits.

In addition to the development of new light sources, the automation of lighthouses and changing user requirements play a significant part in the relevance and size of power supplies.

However, developments in technology have made it possible to reduce the power consumption of AtoN without any detrimental effect on the service provided to mariners. In particular, battery systems, rather than diesel generators, can be used as back up for utility power or as the companion to renewable energy sources. Integrated power system lanterns may also meet the requirements, thus eliminating the need for external power generation and energy storage.

4 USER REQUIREMENTS

The user requirement also has an important part to play in power consumption. For every mile reduction in range for lights the required luminous intensity is roughly halved and hence power consumption reduced. The application of visual and audible AtoN is changing; ranges are being reduced considerably, resulting in far less power demand.

▶AUTOMATION

Automation will reduce the need for constant domestic loads, but is very likely to require the use of control devices to ensure that navigation equipment operates when required. Typical examples are day/night sensing for the light sources, fog detectors for audible signals and load control for diesel generators.

▶DISADVANTAGES

The continual reduction of power consumption and thus the requirement for smaller power supplies has distinct advantages, but when this is applied to buildings that were previously occupied, there are building conditioning issues that should be recognised and addressed. The result could be damp conditions leading

to the deterioration of the building itself as well as the AtoN equipment.

Where mains power is available, heating or air conditioning can be provided without increasing the capacity of back-up power supplies. However, with renewable energy or hybrid operated systems there is likely to be no spare capacity for building conditioning as this would negate any savings made.

In these cases, alternatives need to be considered including:

- improved ventilation;
- good building maintenance;
- ancillary powered heating/cooling either by high efficiency gas or diesel fired boilers, photovoltaic or wind generators;
- high efficiency power, e. g., stirling cycle engine, fuel cell, etc. to provide heating as well as electrical power.

5 SELECTION OF POWER SYSTEMS AND ENERGY STORAGE

This section identifies those items that should be taken into consideration when selecting energy storage and associated power systems for AtoN locations. Table 1-1 provides general guidance on the most appropriate power systems for a number of locations, power requirements and environmental issues. However, it would be prudent to use the appropriate guideline to better determine the potential and define the optimal solution.

Table 1-1 Selection guide of power systems for AtoN

Sources of Energy	Remote Site	No Easy Access	High Power >300 W·h/d	Medium Power 100-300 W·h/d	Low Power <100 W·h/d	Extreme Temperatures	Ventilation not possible	Buoy	Major Floating Aid	Life Expectancy (estimated years)
Utility power	+o	+	++	++	+	++	++	-	-	-
Diesel generator	+	o	+	o	-	o	o	-	-	20
Photovoltaic	++	++	-	+	++	++	-	++	++	20
Wind HAWG *	++	-	+	++	++	o	-	o	+	1 to 15
Wind VAWG * *	++	-	+	++	++	++	-	+	+	10 to 20
Fuel Cell	+	o	+	++	++	o	o	-	+	5 to 10
Wave Actuated Generator	-	-	-	+	++	o	-	+	o	3 to 10

(continued)

Sources of Energy	Remote Site	No Easy Access	High Power >300 W·h/d	Medium Power 100-300 W·h/d	Low Power <100 W·h/d	Extreme Temperatures	Ventilation not possible	Buoy	Major Floating Aid	Life Expectancy (estimated years)
Hybrid	++	++	+	++	+	o	-	++	+	Not applied
++ Recommended solution + Good solution o Not recommended					+o Recommended solution where utility power is available - Not relevant					

* HAWG: Horizontal Axis Wind Generator.

* * VAWG: Vertical Axis Wind Generator.

5.1 GUIDANCE ON POWER SOURCES

Where reliable and readily available power is supplied by others, this may be the cheapest energy source. When utility power is used, it is sufficient, to provide back-up facilities by means of energy storage only. The capacity of the device need only be sufficient to enable time for access to site and repair. Table 1-2 provides information on the practical choice of energy storage systems and guidance on the application of power sources for marine aids to navigation.

Where externally supplied power is difficult or impossible to install, solar energy, wind energy or other renewable source of energy should be considered as the next best option. In some situations, where a renewable energy source is not practicable, primary batteries can be used.

Diesel generators should only be considered for major loads.

Table 1-2 Selection guide of energy storage equipment for AtoN

Energy Storage		Remote Site	Maintenance Required	High Power >300 W·h/d	Medium Power 100-300 W·h/d	Low Power <100 W·h/d	Extreme Temperatures	Ventilation not possible	Buoy	Major Floating Aid	Comments
Secondary Cells	Lead acid	+	Yes	+	+	+	-	o	o	+	
	Sealed Gel lead acid	++	No	+	+	+	+	-	++	+	
	AGM lead acid *	+	No	o	+	+	+	-	+	-	
	Pocket NiCd	++	Yes	+	+	+	+	o	o	+	Charge level dependent

(continued)

Energy Storage		Remote Site	Maintenance Required	High Power >300 W·h/d	Medium Power 100-300 W·h/d	Low Power <100 W·h/d	Extreme Temperatures	Ventilation not possible	Buoy	Major Floating Aid	Comments
Secondary Cells	Sintered NiCd	+	No	+	+	+	+	o	o	+	
	Sealed NiCd	++	No	+	+	+	+	–	++	+	
	Ni-Metal Hydride	+	No	+	+	+	–	–	+	+	
	Lithium (secondary) * *	+	No	+	+	+	–	–	+	+	
Primary Cells	Air depolarised	o	No	–	–	+	o	–	+	o	
	Alkaline	o	No	–	–	+	o	++	+	o	
	Zinc-Carbon	–	No	–	–	+	–	++	+	–	
	Lithium (primary)	+	No	o	o	+	o	++	+	o	
++ Recommended solution; + Good solution; o Not recommended; – No comment											

* AGM: Absorbed Glass Mat.

** Caution must be applied when specifying this battery type as the battery chemistry can vary widely thereby offering differing degrees of performance and safety requirements.

5.2 REDUNDANCY, CAPACITY AND AUTONOMY

Whether redundancy is required in the delivery of a unique AtoN is an organisational decision, usually defined in terms of AtoN importance or category. Equipment demands can be captured and a risk-based analysis done to determine the best solution.

The autonomy of the power systems, being either a primary or secondary back-up power, is determined based on a typical, site specific, engineering life cycle analyses, but needs to take into account the battery characteristic.

Tangible considerations known to impact the "sizing and selection" of energy production and storage equipment can include, but are not limited to:

- power load profile (peaks);
- the availability of renewable energy source (e.g. sun, wind);
- life cycle cost;

- regulatory environment;
- environmental risks impact.

When trying to determine the "sizing and selection" of a solar system see "IALA Guideline 1039: Designing Solar Photovoltaic Power System".

6 LIFE CYCLE MANAGEMENT CONSIDERATIONS

The Life Cycle Management covers from conception to disposal; this is having an increasing impact on the design and selection of equipment, and has a direct link to the overall financial requirements.

6.1 INITIATION PHASE

6.1.1 CAPTURING THE MARINERS REQUIREMENTS

The start of any AtoN project is that a requirement is identified by a maritime entity. This could range from a vague idea to a thoroughly considered approach. When developing the design criteria for the final solution, it is imperative to achieve full and concise design requirements from the initiating body.

6.1.2 CONSIDERATION OF DESIGN OPTIONS

Careful consideration should be given to the "Through Life Costs" of any solution as a low capital cost solution could offer very high running costs and vice versa.

It is therefore important to consider the true overall cost of "Ownership" of the AtoN. This consideration should take into account such issues as maintenance periods, equipment replacement periods and environmental implications, both through life and at end of life disposal therefore, end of life recycling/disposal costs should be considered.

6.2 IMPLEMENTATION AND IN-SERVICE PHASES

During the in-service life of the AtoN equipment, it is important to monitor the performance of the equipment to ensure the protection of the environment. Appropriate measures should be taken to limit the impact of the maintenance activities on the environment.

Maintenance activities should be appropriate to protect the heritage status of

the sites and be compliant with the current regulation, where applicable.

It is recommended that the maintenance requirements be evaluated during the conception phase in a manner to extend the maintenance interval wherever possible.

6.3 DISPOSAL PHASE

The disposal of any equipment has to be considered during the conception phase in order to minimise the impact on the environment.

Disposal of equipment containing hazardous materials is an increasingly important factor and the emphasis must be put on reworking/reusing components to extend life and then the recycling of equipment in preference to disposal. Disposal of non-reusable equipment or components should be limited to the minimum.

It is important to ensure that any disposal of AtoN equipment is done according to current regulations and limits the negative impact on the environment as much as possible.

Consideration should be given to passing on obsolete equipment to a museum, if it might be of interest to future generations.

7 ACRONYMS

AIS	automatic identification system
A·h/d	Ampere hour(s) per day
AtoN	marine aids to navigation
HAWG	horizontal axis wind generator
IALA	International Association of Marine Aids to Navigation and Lighthouse Authorities
Ni	nickel
NiCd	nickel cadmium
RACON	radar beacon
UR	user requirement
W·h/d	Watt hour(s) per day

第 G1067-1 号
航标的总用电负荷

1 引言

当计划为现有的或新的航标（AtoN）供电时，在满足操作要求的前提下，选择能耗最低的设备以满足运行要求是非常可取的。需综合考量用电设备的能耗和效率，包括但不限于：

- 光源和光学设备；
- 无线电航标；
- 音响信号；
- 控制和监测系统。

2 如何使用本导则

本文件是一套导则的一部分，需要结合以下文件阅读（如图 2-1 所示）：

IALA G1067-0 导则：航标及相关设备的电力系统选择；

IALA G1067-2 导则：电源；

IALA G1067-3 导则：航标的电能存储。

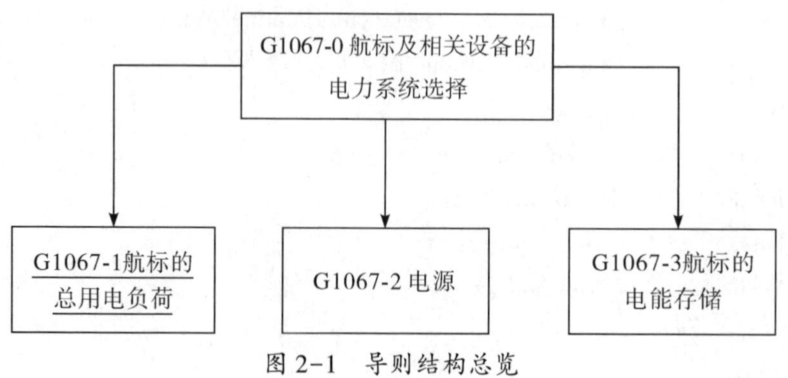

图 2-1　导则结构总览

3 航标负荷总览

确定系统的总用电负荷时，需要考虑以下问题：

- 需要用电的设备有哪些？——识别设备和设备所对应的系统。
- 多少功率？——明确每种操作模式下每个项目的电力消耗。
- 需要多长时间？——了解系统运行期间的所有特性、占空比。
- 何时需要？——掌握日常情况以及不同季节、不同天气、不同交通的需求量，随时调节。

确定总用电负荷的第一步是估算每个负荷运行的时长。负荷运行的时长估算应尽量准确。需要注意的是，如果航标仅在夜间运行，则运行时长应随季节的变化而变化。

估算负荷运行时间的小误差将逐日累积，从而放大全年的误差。这将对高纬度地区航标的安装产生重要的影响。如无详细信息，则可考虑“最坏情况”，并使用按最长冬夜设计的航标系统。

该设计应确保开关装置在符合条件的光照水平下能开、关灯，以匹配计算出的亮灯时长。在较高纬度地区，亮灯时长会受明显的季节性影响。

建议考虑某一航标子系统发生故障时对复杂航标系统的功耗影响。应鼓励制造商公开其所供应的设备最可能的故障模式和相应的功耗情况。

3.1 静态负荷

静态负荷是指设备在静默、侦听或监测时所需的功率。收发机在发送和收听时通常具有不同的载荷配置数据。通常，电子设备在白天通电时，充电控制器的电量消耗比在夜间或电池充满电时多。

3.2 昼夜负荷

日间负荷或夜间负荷会因季节而发生显著变化。例如，在北纬 58 度，一盏夜间工作的灯器在 12 月大约须照明 18 个小时，而在 6 月，照明时间则不到 6 个小时。这些差异可能对电源和电能存储系统的大小产生重大影响。在较高纬度地区，能源效率变得非常重要。例如，航标灯在白天 5 mA 的静默电流似乎不大，但在 60 天的周期内，电池需要额外的 7 A·h 容量以应对静默电流。

3.3 电力需求变化

航标设置点上的电力需求受诸多因素的影响，包括但不限于：

- 温度区域；
- 日间/夜间负荷；
- 纬度；
- 天气条件；
- 设备类型和操作模式；
- 峰值需求。

极端温度和电压波动也可能导致负载的功率需求发生变化。随着电压的增加，电阻负载将消耗更多的能量。许多组件都能表现出这种特性。

当阵列给电池充电时，白天在光伏供电的航标上运行的负载会暴露在更高的系统电压中。使用的组件要能应对这些变化。负载的功耗必须在常规的工作电压下确定。

在经常有厚云或浓雾的地区，设置合适的灯光开、关的阈值非常重要。若关闭阈值太高，则灯器在多云天气时的关闭时间可能会比预期时间延迟数小时，从而导致电池耗尽。

日间和夜间运行的负载可能会有不同的系统电压，因此可能需要计算平均功耗，以准确预测系统性能。同样，有些负载的功耗会随环境中温度的变化而变化。

考虑不同纬度所导致的夜间时长的差异，需要调整负荷需求。在一些纬度地区，需要重点考虑负荷的季节性变化。

厂商提供准确的载荷配置数据和运行条件要求对估算实际电量需求非常有帮助。航标位置的实际测量（或计算值）对电力系统设计的完整性至关重要。

除上述因素外，还须仔细考虑配电基础设施的设计，以确保在不影响设备运行的情况下满足总的瞬时负荷，这对于现代电子化的航标和无线电航标来说越来越重要。

4 日负荷和季节负荷变化

注：本节应结合“IALA G1038 导则：激活航标灯器的方法和环境光照水平”阅读。

4.1　日负荷的计算

一次电池或二次电池供电系统设计中最重要的方面是计算每种设备的日用电负荷（E_{DL}）。这通常表示为瓦时/每天（W·h/d）。

$$E_{DL}=负荷\times 每天运行持续时间$$

公式 1　日负荷的计算

其中：

E_{DL} 为日用电负荷，单位为瓦时（W·h）；负荷是设备的功耗，单位为瓦（W）；持续时间是每天的运行时间，单位为小时（h）。

▶占空比

如果负荷是循环的，上述日负荷计算可通过以下公式修正。

$$占空比=\frac{开启时间}{开启时间+关闭时间}$$

公式 2　占空比

4.2　日负荷的季节性变化

只在白天或夜间运行的日光控制的负载需要做更多的预测工作。因为日照时数每天都在变化，所以，负荷也会每天变化。大多数简单的电力系统设计都是基于最高的日耗电量的。在北半球，最高夜负荷出现在 12 月 21 日左右，而最高昼负荷出现在 6 月 21 日左右。南半球的最高负荷出现日期则正好相反。更精确的方法是创建一个计算机程序或者使用电子数据表，以便计算一年中每天的负荷，然后在运行强度最大的时段对能量平衡进行评估。

假设负载在日出或日落时打开或关闭，确定每日负荷首先要计算日照时数，或者相反，计算夜间时数。$H_{日照}$ 为一天中日出和日落之间的小时数。$H_{夜间}$ 为日落和日出之间的小时数即日照时数。下列公式可用于计算日照时数。应该注意的是，考虑到地球为椭球体和大气折射的影响，该公式采用了近似的计算方法，计算了赤道上最精确的日照时数。有很多计算日照时数的替代方法可以使用，但应根据下列公式或测量值对结果进行检验。

如所有计算都以度为单位，则：

$$H_{日照}=\frac{2}{15}\arccos\frac{-0.0151-\sin L\times\sin D}{\cos L\times\cos D}$$

公式 3　日照时数（度）

其中，$H_{日照}$（日照时数）为日出和日落之间的小时数；L 是所在地的纬度，北纬为正值，南纬为负值；D 为太阳的赤纬，北半球赤纬为正值，南半球赤纬为负值。

注：系数-0.0151 用来表示受地球半径和折射影响的日照时数。

4.2.1 关于赤纬的说明

太阳赤纬的范围在 23.45° S（-23.45°）和 23.45° N（+23.45°）之间。冬至日的夜间时数最大。北半球冬至日的赤纬度为 23.45° S（-23.45°）。南半球冬至日的赤纬度为 23.45° N（+23.45°）。

为了确定公式 3 使用的 D 值，需要根据使用的儒略日期考虑三种不同的情况。太阳赤纬度（D）可以近似为：

$D = 23.45\ \sin\ [1.008\ (n-80)]$　　其中，$n = 1-80$；

$D = 23.45\ \sin\ [0.965\ (n-80)]$　　其中，$n = 81-266$；

$D = -23.45\ \sin\ [0.975\ (n-266)]$　　其中，$n = 267-365$。

其中，n 是儒略日期，所有计算均以度为单位。

4.2.2 关于高纬度的说明

对于纬度大于 65.6°的地区，上述理论计算在一年中的某些时段内存在数学上的不可能，因此，计算以下部分必须用值 1 或-1 代替。日照时数公式的以下部分，

$$\frac{-0.0151-\sin L\times\sin D}{\cos L\times\cos D}$$

在一年的某一段时间内可能小于-1，而在另一段时间内可能大于+1。在一年中，这些时间内的日照时数如下：

若$\dfrac{-0.0151-\sin L\times\sin D}{\cos L\times\cos D}<-1$，则日照时数=24（太阳不落山）；

若$\dfrac{-0.0151-\sin L\times\sin D}{\cos L\times\cos D}>1$，则日照时数=0（太阳不升起）。

日落与日出之间的小时数，即夜间时数，可以利用日照时数轻松算出：

$$H_{\text{夜间}}=24-H_{\text{日照}}。$$

公式 4　夜间时数

4.2.3 运行时数

运行时数通常对应夜间时数（$H_{\text{夜间}}$），但由于不同国家的规定不同，运行时数可能会延长。因此，可以插入校正因子来修正 $H_{\text{夜间}}$。

这是航标灯开启和关闭的一个理论数值。但在实践中，这是通过感光元件来实现的。根据气候条件、当地条件、阴影和感光元件调整，实际数字可能超过这个值。为了应对这些变化，特别是在高纬度地区，可将安全系数

应用于公式。

5 实际负荷

5.1 白炽灯光源

注：在“光源”一节中只讨论白炽灯，LED 在第 5.2 节中讨论。需要检查是否包括其他种类的光源，如有，应修改计算方法。

所有航标最常见的负荷是光源。灯按电压、电流和功率分类。从闪光器或电压调节器接收调节器输出电压的灯消耗额定电流或计算电流。例如，一盏 12 伏 100 瓦的白炽灯在额定电压下电流为 8.33 安。此额定值仅适用于稳态运行的白炽灯。闪光灯在熄灯期间虽然可以节省能耗，但从暗到亮，由于灯丝的冷电流浪涌影响，在闪烁期间消耗的电流会超过额定电流，如图 2-2 所示。

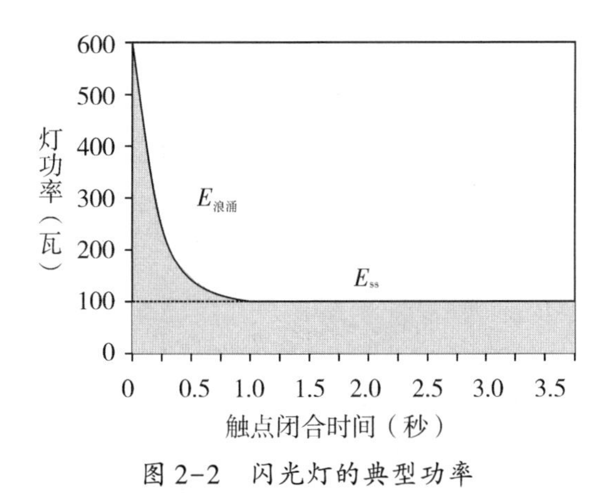

图 2-2　闪光灯的典型功率

曲线下面的面积表示能量（E）。一次闪光所消耗的能量（E_1）可分为两部分：

$$E_1 = E_{浪涌} + E_{ss}$$

公式 5　一次闪光的总能耗

其中，E_1 为一次闪光的能耗；$E_{浪涌}$是与浪涌影响相关的能耗，由图 2-3 中曲线的上部面积表示；E_{ss} 是与稳态功率相关的能耗，由图 2-3 中矩形区域表示。

考虑到 $E_{浪涌}$是相对于任何给定的灯器来说的，因此，$E_{浪涌}$可被视为常量。图 2-3 为白炽灯航标的浪涌系数。

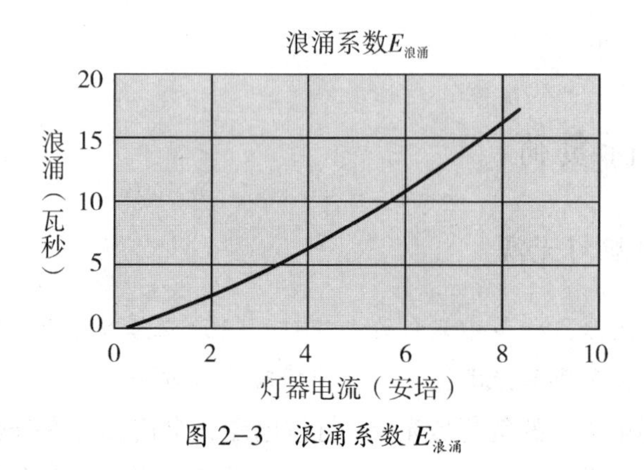

图 2-3　浪涌系数 $E_{浪涌}$

$E_{浪涌}$可通过以下公式来估算：

$$E_{浪涌} = 0.1019 \times I^2 + 1.24 \times I - 0.3341$$

公式 6　估算 $E_{浪涌}$

其中，I 为灯电流，单位为安；$E_{浪涌}$单位为瓦秒。

现在考虑 E_{ss}：

$$E_{ss} = P_{ss} \times T_{闪光}$$

公式 7　与稳态功率相关的能耗

其中，P_{ss} 为灯的稳态功率（瓦），$T_{闪光}$为闪光时长（秒），E_{ss} 单位为瓦秒。

要计算一天的能耗（即日负荷），将其乘以一天的闪光次数：

$$E_{DL} = E_1 \times \frac{H}{T_{周期}}$$

公式 8　来自闪光能耗的日能量负荷

其中，E_1 为每次闪光消耗的能量，单位为瓦秒，其中，$E_1 = E_{浪涌} + E_{ss}$；H 为灯器每天运行时数（小时）；$T_{周期}$是灯器的闪光周期（开加关时间）（秒）。注意，日负荷 E_{DL} 可方便地以瓦时/天的单位计算出来。

将公式 6 和公式 7 代入到公式 8 中，可得：

$$E_{DL} = \left(E_{浪涌} + E_{ss}\right) \times \frac{H}{T_{周期}}$$

公式 9　闪光灯的单日总能量

上述灯器能量是基于经验数据的近似值计算的，可用于代替实际测量，灯器供应商应提供所有常用的闪光器节奏所对应的平均电流值，可利用该数据对日负荷进行更简明的计算。

注：这些浪涌效应随着灯质中闪光数的增加而减弱。

5.2　LED 光源

产生可见光的原理不同，用于驱动发光二极管（LED）的电路的复杂程度也不同。这些驱动方法示例如下：

- 无源电源电路；
- 有源电源电路；
- 开关电源电路。

在航标分站进行系统集成过程中需要注意 LED 光源供电可能会产生一些问题。例如，任何 LED 灯器都可能成为电磁干扰（EMI）的来源，也可能受来自其他设备的电磁干扰。

由输入功率控制的 LED 阵列或单个 LED 光源的功耗计算与白炽灯类似，但 LED 光源没有像图 2-2 中反映的高起动电流，而且根据实践，$E_{浪涌}$趋于零。

▶复合 LED 光源

许多现代复合 LED 光源是由几个子系统组成的，将 LED、闪光器、GPS 接收机、测量和监测模块集成在一个单一电源供电的设备中。在这种情况下，应根据制造商提供的应用场景中可能出现的所有电源模式信息进行设备功耗预算计算。

大多数情况下，LED 集成在一个灯器中，该灯器包含一个集成的 LED 电源和一个闪光器，通常被称为独立灯器。此类设备的功耗可分为闪时功耗、闪间功耗和日间静态功耗。

$$E_{DL} = \left[P_{fl}(瓦) \times \frac{T_{闪光}}{T_{周期}} + P_{bfl}(瓦) \times \left(1 - \frac{T_{闪光}}{T_{周期}}\right)\right] \times H_{夜间}\left(\frac{小时}{天}\right) + P_{idle}(瓦)\left[24 - H_{夜间}\left(\frac{小时}{天}\right)\right]$$

公式 10　复合 LED 光源的日负荷

其中，E_{DL} 为日负荷，单位为瓦时/天；P_{fl} 为闪时功耗，单位为瓦；P_{bfl} 为闪间功耗，单位为瓦；P_{idle} 为日间静态功耗，单位为瓦；$H_{夜间}$是夜间时数（或每天的运行时数）。

要计算出一天的耗电量（日负荷），需要一些额外的数据：$T_{周期}$为灯器的闪光周期（秒）；$T_{闪光}$为闪光周期内的总亮光时间（秒）。

5.3 金属卤化物灯

金属卤化物放电灯只用于旋转光学元器件中，需要对应的镇流器放电撞击并维持灯的电离电弧。这些镇流器单元的消耗可能会超过灯的额定功耗，所以在确定负荷大小时必须算上镇流器的功耗。同样，应咨询制造商以确定额定系统电压和温度下的功率需求，这些值应通过对实际装置的测量来确认。

$$E_{DL} = P_{lb}(\text{瓦}) \times \text{每天运行小时数}(\text{小时/天})$$

公式11　旋转光学元件的日负荷

其中，E_{DL}为日负荷，单位为瓦时/天；P_{lb}为灯器和镇流器功耗的测量值/出厂参数，单位为瓦。

5.4 闪光器/控制器

用于闪光或控制光源的装置也需要电源。闪光器/控制器的制造商应能提供其装置的功率需求信息，平均值应满足高效率装置。否则，可能需要根据闪烁、闪间、空闲（白天）的要求来计算负载曲线。一般来说，能源需求按日负荷计算，如下所示：

$$E_{DL(\text{平均})} = P_q \times H_{\text{日照}} + P_{bfl} \times (1 - \text{占空比}) \times H_{\text{夜间}} + P_{fl} \times \text{占空比} \times H_{\text{夜间}}$$

公式12　闪光器的日负荷

其中，E_{DL}为日负荷，单位为瓦时/天；P_q为白天闲时静态功耗，单位为瓦；$H_{\text{日照}}$为每天日照时数，单位为小时/天；P_{bfl}为闪间功耗，单位为瓦；$H_{\text{夜间}}$为夜间时数（或每天的运行时间）；P_{fl}为闪时功耗，单位为瓦。

5.5 旋转光学元件

旋转光学元件的负荷与旋转转盘组件的构件相关。灯塔上通常会使用连续旋转转盘，昼夜工作，以防止太阳通过透镜反聚焦烧毁灯器或换灯机。因此，回旋机构和控制系统的功率要求应作为连续负荷。此负荷可能受温度影响产生很大变化，因此，在向制造商索要电力需求信息时，请务必确定运行环境。

$$E_{DL} = P_{\text{电机}}(\text{瓦}) \times \text{每天运行小时数}(\text{小时/天})$$

公式13　旋转光学元件的日负荷

其中，E_{DL}为日负荷，单位为瓦时/天；$P_{\text{电机}}$为电机和控制系统功耗，单位为瓦。

旋转信标可能使用常开式闪光器来调节电压并操作换灯器，能源需求为：

$$E_{DL}=[P_{灯光}(瓦)\times H_{夜间}(小时/天)]+E_{闪光器}(瓦时/天)+E_{电机}(瓦时/天)$$

公式 14　旋转光学元件和光源的日负荷

5.6　音响信号

音响信号可在较宽的电压和温度范围内工作，需要信号制造商提供预期工作电压和预期工作温度下的能耗需求。

$$E_{DL}=[P_{爆震}(瓦)\times 占空比+P_{静默}(瓦)\times(1-占空比)]\times 运行小时数/天$$

公式 15　音响信号的日负荷

其中，E_{DL}为日负荷，单位为瓦时/天；$P_{爆震}$是爆震期间的音响信号和驱动系统功耗，单位为瓦；$P_{静默}$是静默时的音响信号和驱动器系统功耗，单位为瓦；占空比为一个周期内爆震时长和周期之比，以十进制值表示。

要预测能见度探测器控制下的音响信号的运行时间，需要参考低能见度的历史时数数据。

5.7　能见度探测器

能见度探测器可以用来减少音响信号的噪声污染。这些设备可能会在探照仪和接收机窗口中使用加热器，以防止在寒冷的天气中发生冷凝。加热器开启时的温度因型号而异。操作人员必须确定这些加热器的开启温度，并获取该区域的温度数据，从而确定加热器的激活时间（占空比）。数据记录器是确定加热器占空比的实用工具，但是由于负荷持续增加，不考虑严寒情况可能会导致电力系统过早故障。数据记录器还可提供音响信号剩余工作时间数据。

$$E_{DL}=P_{加热器}(瓦)\times 占空比\times 24\ 小时/天+P_{探照仪}(瓦)\times 占空比\times 24\ 小时/天$$

公式 16　能见度探测器的日负荷

其中，E_{DL}为日负荷，单位为瓦时/天；$P_{加热器}$是加热器功耗，单位为瓦；占空比是开启时间和总周期之间的比率，以十进制值表示；$P_{探照仪}$是传感头和控制系统每天的功耗。

5.8　控制和监测系统

5.8.1　控制设备

用于控制航标的设备通常也耗电。一般来说，系统正常运行时（即主航标可运行并使用主电源系统）的功耗是额定的。与这些装置相关的负荷按连续负荷计算。

$$E_{DL}=P_{运行}(瓦)\times 运行小时数+P_{待机}(瓦)\times 运行小时数$$

公式 17　控制系统的日负荷

其中，E_{DL} 为日负荷，单位为瓦时/天；$P_{运行}$ 为航标运行时，所有运行设备的功耗单位为瓦；$P_{待机}$ 是非日常运行的所有备用设备的功耗，单位为瓦。

5.8.2　监测系统

通过太阳能设备供电的低能耗监测系统在复杂程度、传输方式和电力需求方面存在很大差异，并且数据传输方式将极大地影响电力需求，有线、无线和卫星链路对电源需求各不相同。在数据传输过程中，它们可能会使用较大功率。应建立严格的机制来控制链路运行的时间，但如果数据传输设备一天短暂传输一次或两次，通常可以忽略其功率需求。在这种情况下，可将静态需求按连续负荷计算得出日负荷。许多监测系统允许从监测中心进行访问，而操作员从外部过度请求数据可能会导致能量消耗超过设计参数。操作人员可咨询设备制造商以确定所选设备的实际功耗，但建议以现场测量得到的数据为准。

因此，可推导出监测系统静态待机负载及其根据预计占空比进入增强通信模式收发数据时的负载如下：

$$E_{DL}=P_{通信}(瓦)\times 占空比\times 24\ 小时/天+P_{静态}(瓦)\times(1-占空比)\times 24\ 小时/天$$

公式 18　监测系统的日负荷

其中，E_{DL} 为日负荷，单位为瓦时/天；$P_{通信}$ 为数据交换期间的功耗，单位为瓦；占空比是总通信时间与 24 小时周期之间的比率，以十进制值表示；$P_{静态}$ 为每天的静态持续功耗。

监测单元还附带额外的功能，如 GPS 信号接收和闪烁同步、测量等。因此，建议操作人员在考虑所有相关因素（如环境温度、电源电压和与岸站的距离等）的情况下，为产品在特定工作状态下建立相应的功耗曲线。

5.9　充电控制器

充电控制器用于管理从能源到电池储能系统的能量和充电状况。可提供过充保护、过放保护和光伏系统的反向电流保护。充电控制器对效率和静态功率都有要求，制造商所使用的效率数据是太阳能阵列的调节器控制

的可变功率，通常是满载效率的 98%。因为能量损失不恒定且随充电需求而变化，所以，充电控制器的负载被定义为 IALA 太阳能组件、航标灯激活以及环境光照水平的一个影响因子（即电池效率）。

“IALA 1039 导则：航标太阳能发电系统设计（太阳能测量工具）”只保留了控制器的静态负载，且通常被认为是一个小于 20 mA 的常数。

$$E_{DL} = P_{静态}(瓦) \times H_{运行}(小时/天)$$

公式 19　充电控制器的日负荷

其中，E_{DL} 为日负荷，单位为瓦时/天；$P_{静态}$ 为每天的静态持续功耗；$H_{运行}$ 为每天的运行时数。

5.10　AIS

5.10.1　概述

AIS 具有取代或提升现有遥测遥控系统的潜力，且本身具备提供导航标服务的能力。具体参阅“IALA A-126 建议案：船舶自动识别系统（AIS）在航标中的应用”。

AIS 航标的功耗取决于其使用类型（1 型、2 型或 3 型）及设备单元的参数设置。以下这些参数设置经过优化，可最大限度地降低功耗。

- VDL 接入方法：FATDMA 功耗比 RATDMA 更低；
- FATDMA 时隙选择：信道 A 和信道 B 时隙应及时一同闭合，以尽量缩短 AIS 航标工作的周期（假设使用推荐模式 B）；
- 报告间隔：延长报告时间间隔可减少功耗，但是时间间隔应满足“IALA A-126 建议案”的要求①；
- AIS 航标应设计或配置成在非运行时间进入“睡眠”模式；
- 传输的消息的数量和类型；
- 射机功率。

5.10.2　电力需求的计算

可使用以下公式估算发送 21 号助航报文和 6 号遥测报文的 AIS 航标的功率需求：

① 在 AIS 航标的报告间隔期间，本地 AIS 基站重复 AIS 航标消息可能会延长 AIS 航标单元的报告间隔。例如，AIS 航标可能有 10 分钟的报告间隔，但是本地 AIS 基站每帧（即每分钟）重复 AIS 航标消息。

▶RATDMA 运行

$$E_{RX}=[P_s+(T_s+60)(P_w-P_s)/T_r]\times 24 \text{ 瓦时/天}$$

公式 20　RATDMA 运行的功率要求

其中，E_{RX} 为休眠或等待传输时的功耗；P_s 为设备休眠时的功率（瓦）；T_s 为设备在唤醒后获取时隙图谱所用的时间（秒）；P_w 为设备在唤醒但未传输时所消耗的功率（瓦）；T_r 为报告间隔（秒）。

$$E_{T21}=P_t\times\frac{4}{2250}\times\frac{60}{T_r}\times 24 \text{ 瓦时/天}$$

$$E_{T6}=P_t\times\frac{2}{2250}\times\frac{60}{T_m}\times 24 \text{ 瓦时/天}$$

$$E_{DL}=E_{RX}+E_{T21}+E_{T6} \text{ 瓦时/天}$$

公式 21　发送 21 和 6 号报文的 AIS 装置的功耗估算

其中，E_{T21} 为 21 号助航报文传输的功耗；P_t 为设备传输时所消耗的功率，单位为瓦；T_r 为报告间隔（秒）；E_{T6} 为 6 号遥测报文传输的功耗；T_m 为 6 号遥测报文的报告间隔（秒）；E_{DL} 为日负荷。

5.10.3　FATDMA 运行

使用与上述相同的公式，但参数 T_s 为 GPS 接收器在唤醒后获得固定位置所需的时间（如安装了 DGPS 接收器，则 T_s 将是唤醒后获得修正的 DGPS 位置所需的时间）。

注意：当使用 FATDMA 模式时，因为不需要为甚高频接收器供电，P_w 将显著降低。

5.11　雷康

雷康的功耗难以预测，因为负载将由雷康被激发的次数确定。为避免因停泊船只的雷达处于开启状态或因航道异常繁忙而持续激发应答器，大多数雷康对广播的响应次数均设置了上限。请咨询制造商，了解这些设备的高、中、低功率需求值，以及咨询该地区的引航员，确定水路中的交通状况，或在最大通信量期间，用电能表或电度表进行为期 2 个月的能量需求测量，以获得实际负载信息。

$$E_{DL}=[P_t(\text{瓦})\times\text{占空比}+P_q(\text{瓦})\times(1-\text{占空比})]\times 24 \text{ 小时/天}$$

公式 22　雷康的日负荷

其中，E_{DL} 为日负荷，单位为瓦时/天；P_t 为设备传输时所消耗的功率，单位为瓦；P_q 为设备在传输周期之间所消耗的功率，单位为瓦；占空比是

总传输时间与 24 小时周期之间的比率，以十进制值表示。

6 其他负载

6.1 非重要负载

非重要负载，如生活照明，最好能处于自动控制的形式之下，以确保它们不会被长期接通在电源系统上进行电量消耗。对此类非重要负载应配备独立的电池系统，并调整电池系统大小以满足运行要求。

6.2 季节性助航设备

季节性助航设备在一年中的部分时间内运行，在非运行期间将被移除或关闭。

建议操作人员要确保长时间断电的设备不包含内部储能单元。非运行期间，这种储能单元为记忆存储单元供能以备份可能丢失关键的信息。此外，当通过遥控供电时，操作人员应确保通电后此类设备不会产生过多的能耗。

7 结论

一旦每个负载被充分表征，为确保系统能量平衡，须计算每个白天和夜晚的负载总和，以确定每日能源需求、电池每日最低剩余电量和每季度最低剩余电量。

对于太阳能系统的设计，这些总负载的应用可参照《航标灯激活的方法及环境光水平》要求进行，可参照“IALA G1039 导则：设计航标太阳能发电系统（太阳能测量工具）”以开展有效的太阳能设计。

针对日负荷（E_{DL}）的量，操作者可通过计算进行保守的系统设计。使用设计程序计算每天的 E_{DL}，并将其与电池容量或可再生能源产生的能量进行比较，可设计一个效率更高的系统。

要成功估算能源需求，最关键的因素是：

- 总负荷的定义；
- 负荷特性的定义。

8 缩略语

A·h	ampere hour(s)（安时）
AIS	automatic identification system（船舶自动识别系统）
AtoN	marine aid(s) to navigation（航海辅助标志，简称“航标”）
D	Suns declination angle（太阳赤纬，单位“度”）
DGPS	differential global positioning system（差分全球定位系统）
°C	degrees centigrade（摄氏度）
FATDMA	fixed-access time-division multiple access（固定接入时分多址）
GPS	global position system（全球定位系统）
h/d	hours per day（小时每天）
L	latitude（纬度，单位“度”）
LED	light emitting diode（发光二极管）
mA	milliampere（毫安）
mW	milliwatt（毫瓦）
n	number of the day in the Julian calendar（儒略历中的日数）
N	north（北）
RACON	radar beacon（雷达信标，音译“雷康”）
RATDMA	random access time division multiple access（随机接入时分多址）
s	second（秒）
S	south（南）
V	Volt(s)（伏特）
VDL	VHF data link（甚高频数据链路）
W	Watt(s)（瓦）
W·h/d	Watt hours per day（瓦时/天）
W·s	Watt seconds（瓦秒）

附件 A　日照时数公式的进一步解析

推导从下列基本天文公式开始。

$$\cos\theta_h = \cos L\cos D\cos\omega + \sin L\sin D$$

公式 23　入射角

其中，θ_h 为太阳射线在水平表面上的入射角（天顶距或太阳光线）与垂直线之间的角度；L 为测量点纬度；D 为太阳赤纬；ω 为时角（注：所有角度单位均为度）。

由公式 23 得出：

$$\omega = \arccos\frac{\cos\theta_h - \sin L\times\sin D}{\cos L\times\cos D}$$

公式 24　时角

日出被定义为太阳上边缘可见时的时间。日出时，太阳的中心在地平线呈 52′的弧度，其中太阳的半径与地平线呈 16′的弧夹角，但由于大气折射的影响，又增加了 36′的弧度。因此，在公式 24 中，$\theta_h = 90°52'$时，将出现日出。在公式 24 中设置 $\theta_h = 90°52'$即可计算时角 $\omega_{日出}$：

$$\omega_{日出} = \arccos\frac{\cos 90°52' - \sin L\times\sin D}{\cos L\times\cos D} = \arccos\frac{-0.0151 - \sin L\times\sin D}{\cos L\times\cos D}$$

公式 25　日出时的时角

日出到当地正午之间的时间量是将 ω 转换为时间（经度中 15°弧对应 1 小时）得到的：

$$H_{日出-正午} = \omega_{日出}/15°$$

其中，$H_{日出-正午}$单位为小时。

从日出到日落的时间是从日出到当地正午时间的两倍：

$$H_{日出-日落} = 2\omega_{日出}/15°$$

公式 26　日出到日落的时间–度

结合公式 25 和公式 26：

$$= \frac{2}{15}\arccos\frac{-0.0151 - \sin L\times\sin D}{\cos L\times\cos D}$$

公式 27　日出到日落的时间

附件 B 运用示例

B 1 日负荷计算

例如，对于 1 瓦的连续负载，该计算表示为（参见公式 1）：

$$E_{DL} = \text{负荷} \times \text{每天运行持续时间} = 1\ \text{瓦} \times 24\ \text{时} = 24\ \text{瓦时/天}$$

这意味着运行时电源每天需提供 24 瓦时的电力。

B 2 占空比计算

24 小时运行，亮 3 秒、灭 3 秒，1 瓦的循环日负荷表示为每日负荷（参见公式 2）：

$$E_{DL} = 1\ \text{瓦} \times 24\ \text{时/天} \times \frac{3\ \text{秒亮}}{3\ \text{秒亮}+3\ \text{秒灭}} = 12\ \text{瓦时/天}$$

通过循环负载，在这种情况下的日负荷是 100%的占空比运行负荷的一半，这是节约能源的一个重要方面。

B 3 夜间时数计算

要算出在北纬 42 度，亮 3 秒、灭 3 秒，只在夜间运行的 1 瓦的循环负荷的最大日负荷，进行如下操作：

由于负荷在夜间运行，最大日负荷出现在冬至，此时的太阳偏角为 −23.45°，即 $D = -23.45°$，所有计算以度为单位（参见公式 3）：

$$H_{\text{日照}} = \frac{2}{15}\arccos\frac{-0.0151-\sin(42)\times\sin(-23.45°)}{\cos L(42)\times\cos(-23.45)} = 9.1\ \text{小时/天}$$

已知：

$$H_{\text{夜间}} = 24 - H_{\text{日照}} = 24 - 9.1 = 14.9\ \text{小时/天}$$

因此，最大日负荷（E_{DL}）为：

$$E_{DL} = 1\ \text{瓦} \times 14.9\ \text{小时/天} \times \frac{3\ \text{秒亮}}{3\ \text{秒亮}+3\ \text{秒灭}} = 7.45\ \text{瓦时/天}$$

$D = 23.45\sin[1.008\ (n-80)]$，其中，$n = 45$（2 月 14 日的儒略历日期为 45）。

为确定与 2 月 14 日相同循环负载的日负荷，按以下步骤进行（$D = -13.54°$），计算单位均为度：

$$H_{日照} = \frac{2}{15}\arccos\frac{-0.0151 - \sin(42) \times \sin(-13.54°)}{\cos(42) \times \cos(-13.54°)} = 10.5 \text{ 小时/天}$$

已知：

$$H_{夜间} = 24 - H_{日照} = 24 - 10.5 = 13.5 \text{ 小时/天}$$

因此，日负荷为：

$$E_{DL} = 1 \text{ 瓦} \times 13.5 \text{ 小时/天} \times \left(\frac{3 \text{ 秒亮}}{3 \text{ 秒亮} + 3 \text{ 秒灭}}\right) = 6.75 \text{ 瓦时/天}$$

B 4　闪光白炽灯日负荷计算

一盏 1.15 安（13.8 瓦）的灯，一天中的夜间时数为 13.9 小时，亮 1 秒、灭 1 秒，日负荷是多少？使用公式 9：

$$E_{DL} = (E_{浪涌} + E_{ss}) \times \frac{H_{夜间}}{T_{周期}}$$

使用公式 6 计算 $E_{浪涌}$，其中，$I = 1.15$ 安，

$$E_{浪涌} = 0.1019 \times I^2 + 1.24 \times I - 0.3341 = 0.1019 \times 1.15^2 + 1.24 \times 1.15 - 0.3341$$

$$E_{浪涌} = 1.2 \text{ 瓦秒}$$

根据公式 6 计算 E_{ss}，其中，$P_{ss} = 13.8$ 瓦和 $T_{闪光} = 1$ 秒，

$$E_{ss} = 13.8 \times 1$$

根据公式 6 计算 E_{DL}，其中，$H_{夜间} = 13.9$ 小时/天，$T_{周期} = 2$ 秒，

$$E_{DL} = (1.2 + 13.8) \times \frac{13.9 \text{ 小时}}{2 \text{ 秒}} = 104 \text{ 瓦时/天}$$

B 5　闪光 LED 灯日负荷计算

一盏 2 瓦的 LED 灯，一天中的夜间时数 13.9，亮 0.5 秒、灭 2.5 秒，日负荷是多少？闪间功耗为 150 mW，静态功耗为 10 mW。使用公式 10：

$$E_{DL} = \left[P_{fl} \times \frac{T_{闪光}}{T_{周期}} + P_{bfl} \times \left(1 - \frac{T_{闪光}}{T_{周期}}\right)\right] \times H_{夜间} + P_{idle}\ (24 - H_{夜间})$$

其中，$P_{fl} = 2$ W，$P_{bfl} = 0.15$ W，$P_{idle} = 0.01$ W，$H_{夜间} = 13.9$ h，$T_{周期} = 3$ s，$T_{闪光} = 0.5$ s。

$$E_{DL} = \left[2 \times \frac{0.5}{3} + 0.15 \times \left(1 - \frac{0.5}{3}\right)\right] \times 13.9 + 0.01\ (24 - 13.9) = (0.333 +$$

$$0.125) \times 13.9 + 0.101 \approx 6.5 \text{ 瓦时/天}$$

这个例子表明，在低功率 LED 灯中，闪间功耗可能是日总负荷的重要

组成部分。

B 6 闪光器/控制器日负荷计算

使用平均功率数据对控制系统进行简单计算的示例见公式 12：

$$E_{DL(平均)} = P_{平均} \times H_{运行}$$

其中，$E_{DL(平均)}$ 是每天的平均日负荷，单位为瓦时/天；$P_{平均}$是来自制造商数据的控制系统平均持续功率，单位为瓦，为 240 mW；$H_{运行}$是每天运行时数。

$$E_{DL} = 0.24 \times 24 = 5.8 \text{ 瓦时/天}$$

通过将闪光器（示例 B 4）和控制器（见上文）的能量需求结合起来获得系统总能量需求，得到以下结果：

$$E_{DL(总)} = 104 + 5.8 = 109.8 \text{ 瓦时/天}$$

B 7 旋转光学元件日负荷计算

例如，带有 2.03 安 12 伏灯和固定节奏闪光器的旋转信标和带有 1.2 W 连续电机，在北纬 42 度夜间运行，其能量需求为：

使用公式 13：

$$E_{DL} = P_{电机}(\text{瓦}) \times \text{每天运行小时数}(\text{小时/天})$$

其中，E_{DL}为日负荷，单位为瓦时/天；$P_{电机}$是电机和控制系统功耗，单位为瓦。

$$E_{DL} = 1.2(\text{瓦}) \times 24(\text{小时/天}) = 28.8 \text{ 瓦时/天}$$

旋转信标可通过使用固定式闪光器来调节电压并操作换灯器，那么，能源需求是：

$$E_{DL} = [P_{灯}(\text{瓦}) \times H_{夜间}](\text{小时/天}) + E_{闪光器}(\text{瓦时/天}) + E_{电机}(\text{瓦时/天})$$

其中，E_{DL} 为日负荷，单位为瓦时/天；$P_{灯}$ 为灯的功耗，单位为瓦；$H_{夜间}$为每天的夜间时数；$E_{闪光器}$是灯闪光器或控制系统的日能量，单位为瓦时/天；$E_{电机}$是光电机和控制系统的日能量，单位为瓦时/天。

由上可得：$P_{灯} = 24.4$ 瓦，来自上述数据；$H_{夜间} = 14.9$ 小时/天，来自示例 B 3 的夜间时数计算；$E_{闪光器} = 5.8$ 瓦时/天，来自示例 B 6 的闪光器/控制器的日负荷计算。

假设昼夜电源需求相同，

$$E_{DL} = (24.4 \times 14.9) + 5 + 28.8 = 398.16 \text{ 瓦时/天}$$

B 8　音响信号负荷计算

例如，爆震功耗为 21.6 瓦，在静默状态下功耗为 0.24 瓦，每 30 秒有一次 3 秒的爆震节奏，每天工作 6 小时，音响信号的能量需求为：

使用公式 15：

$$E_{DL} = [P_{爆震}(瓦) \times 占空比 + P_{静默}(瓦) \times (1-占空比)] \times 运行小时数/天$$

其中，E_{DL} 为日负荷，单位为瓦时/天；$P_{爆震}$是爆震期间的音响信号和驱动系统功耗，单位为瓦；$P_{静默}$是静默时的音响信号和驱动器系统功耗，单位为瓦；占空比为一个周期内爆震时长和周期之比，以十进制值表示。

$$占空比 = \frac{3\ 秒开}{3\ 秒开 + 27\ 秒关} = 0.10\ 或\ 10\%$$

$$E_{DL} = [21.6(瓦) \times 0.1 + 0.24(瓦) \times (1-0.1)] \times 6 = 14.256\ 瓦时/天$$

B 9　能见度探测器负荷计算

例如，能见度探测器的功率需求为 6 瓦，加热器负荷为 24 瓦。环境温度低于 10 ℃时，加热器打开。该区域的温度数据表明，11 月至 3 月期间的平均最低温度低于 10 ℃，估计在此期间的一半时间内，它们将被激活。能源需求为：

使用公式 16：

$$E_{DL} = P_{加热器}(瓦) \times 占空比 \times 24\ 小时/天 + P_{探照仪}(瓦) \times 占空比 \times 24\ 小时/天$$

公式28　能见度探测器的日负荷

其中，E_{DL} 为日负荷，单位为瓦时/天；$P_{加热器}$是加热器功耗，单位为瓦；占空比是开启时间和总周期之间的比率，以十进制值表示；$P_{探照仪}$是传感头和控制系统每天的功耗。

$$E_{DL(11月-3月)} = 24(瓦) \times 0.5 \times 24\ 小时/天 + 6(瓦) \times 1.0 \times 24\ 小时/天 = 432\ 瓦时/天$$

$$E_{DL(4月-10月)} = 6(瓦) \times 1.0 \times 24\ 小时/天 = 144\ 瓦时/天$$

B 10　控制和监测系统

例如，典型的 12 V 遥测系统的静态电流为 110 mA，并连续监测所有输入。在状态改变时，该设备将给调制解调器供电，并与监测中心通信。通信通常持续 3 分钟，在此期间，设备电流增加到 305 mA。通常情况下，该设备每天通信 12 次。

使用公式 18：

$$E_{DL}=P_{通信}(瓦)\times 占空比\times 24\ 小时/天+P_{静态}(瓦)\times(1-占空比)\times 24\ 小时/天$$

<u>**公式 29　监测系统的日负荷**</u>

其中，E_{DL} 为日负荷，单位为瓦时/天；$P_{通信}$是典型数据交换期间的功耗，单位为瓦；占空比是总通信时间与 24 小时周期之间的比率，以十进制值表示；$P_{静态}$是每天的静态持续功耗。

$$E_{DL}=P_{通信}(瓦)\times 占空比\times 24\ 小时/天+P_{静态}(瓦)\times(1-占空比)\times 24\ 小时/天$$

$$E_{DL}=3.66(瓦)\times 0.025\times 24\ 小时/天+1.32(瓦)\times(1-0.025)\times 24\ 小时/天=2.196+30.88=33.084\ 瓦时/天$$

B 11　充电控制器负载计算

例如，太阳能发电系统上，一个小型充电控制器在满载时的峰值效率为 96%，在 24 伏系统上的静态电流为 10 毫安。该系统的能源需求如下：

使用公式 19：

$$E_{DL}=P_{静态}(瓦)\times H_{运行}(小时/天)$$

<u>**公式 30　充电控制器的日负荷**</u>

其中，E_{DL} 为日负荷，单位为瓦时/天；$P_{静态}$是每天的静态持续功耗；$H_{运行}$是每天的运行时数。

$$E_{DL}=0.24(瓦)\times 24(小时/天)=0.576\ 瓦时/天$$

B 12　使用 RATDMA 访问的 AIS 负荷计算

例如，安装在浮标上的 AIS 装置的休眠电力需求为 12 mW，每 3 分钟唤醒一次，在此期间电力需求为 0.6 W。然后，该设备需要 4 秒钟来确定要传输的时隙。设备在信道 A、B 上传输，传输功率为 30 W。

使用公式 20：

$$E_{RX}=[P_s+(T_s+60)(P_w-P_s)/T_r]\times 24\ 瓦时/天$$

公式 31　RATDMA 运行的功率要求

其中，P_s 为设备休眠时的功率（瓦）；T_s 为设备在唤醒后获取时隙图所用的时间（秒）；P_w 是设备在唤醒但未传输时所消耗功率（瓦）；T_r 为报告间隔（秒）。

$$E_{RX}=[P_s+(T_s+60)(P_w-P_s)/T_r]\times 24\ 瓦时/天$$

$$E_{RX}=[0.012+(4+60)(0.6-0.012)/180]\times 24\ 瓦时/天=5\ 瓦时/天$$

21 号报文能量需求为：

$$E_{T21}=P_t\times\frac{4}{2250}\times\frac{60}{T_r}\times 24\ 瓦时/天$$

$$E_{T21}=30\times\frac{4}{2250}\times\frac{60}{180}\times 24\ 瓦时/天=0.43\ 瓦时/天$$

6 号报文能量需求为：

$$E_{T6}=P_t\times\frac{2}{2250}\times\frac{60}{T_m}\times 24\ 瓦时/天$$

$$E_{T6}=30\times\frac{2}{2250}\times\frac{60}{180}\times 24\ 瓦时/天=0.213\ 瓦时/天$$

总日负荷：

$$E_{DL}=E_{RX}+E_{T21}+E_{T6}\ 瓦时/天$$

公式 32　发送 21 号报文和 6 号报文的 AIS 装置的功耗估算

其中，E_{DL} 为日负荷，E_{RX} 为休眠或等待传输时的功耗，E_{T21} 为 21 号报文传输的功耗，E_{T6} 为 6 号报文传输的功耗。

$$E_{DL}=E_{RX}+E_{T21}+E_{T6}\ 瓦时/天=5+0.43+0.213\ 瓦时/天=5.643\ 瓦时/天$$

B 13　雷康负荷计算

下列计算是基于单个制造商的典型示例，在计算负荷时必须适当考虑设备制造商的数据。

例如，雷康在空闲时的静态电流功率为 24 mW，在传输信号时功率为 8.4 W，占空比限制为 50%。因此，作为最坏的情况，如果连续激发雷康：

使用公式 22：

$$E_{DL}=[P_t(瓦)\times 占空比+P_q(瓦)\times(1-占空比)]\times 24\ 小时/天$$

公式 33　雷康的日负荷

其中，E_{DL} 为日负荷，单位为瓦时/天；P_t是设备传输时的功耗，单位为瓦；P_q是设备在传输周期之间的功耗，单位为瓦；占空比是总传输时间与24小时周期之间的比率，以十进制值表示。

E_{DL} = [P_t(瓦)×占空比+P_q(瓦)×(1−占空比)]×24 小时/天

E_{DL} = [8.4(瓦)×0.5+0.024(瓦)×(1−0.5)]×24 小时/天 = 101.1 瓦时/天

B 14　季节性航标负荷计算

计算负荷需求。一个在42°N下运行的季节性浮标，带有一个1.15安、在夜间以FL6（0.6）节奏运行的灯，在4月1日至10月31日之间使用，其能量需求如下：

根据第4.2节，计算日历限值的太阳赤纬（D）：

$D_{4.1} = 23.45\sin[0.965(91-80)] = 4.320°$

$D_{10.31} = 23.45\sin[0.95(308-266)] = 14.125°$

使用公式3，代入上面的D值和纬度的L值，计算日照时数，从而计算夜间时数。

$$H_{日照4.1} = \frac{2}{15}\arccos\frac{-0.015-\sin 42°\times\sin 4.32°}{\cos 42°\times\cos 4.32°} = 12.7\ 小时/天$$

$H_{夜间4.1}$ = 24 小时/天 − $H_{日照4.1}$ = 24 小时/天 − 12.7 小时/天 = 11.3 小时/天

$$H_{日照10.31} = \frac{2}{15}\arccos\frac{-0.015-\sin 42°\times\sin 14.125°}{\cos 42°\times\cos 14.125°} = 10.4\ 小时/天$$

$H_{夜间10.31}$ = 24 小时/天 − $H_{日照10.31}$ = 24 小时/天 − 10.4 小时/天 = 13.6 小时/天

因此，夜间负荷将在10月31日达到最高值。

然后，用公式9计算平均能源需求：

$$E_{灯} = (E_{浪涌} + P_{ss}\times T_{闪光})\times\frac{H_{夜间}}{T_{周期}}$$

$$E_{灯} = (1.2\ 瓦秒 + 13.8\ 瓦\times 1\ 秒)\times\frac{13.6\ 小时/天}{6\ 秒} = 34.0\ 瓦时/天$$

其中，$E_{浪涌}$ = 1.2 瓦秒；P_{ss} = 13.8 瓦；$T_{闪光}$ = 1 秒；$H_{夜间}$ = 13.6 小时/天；$T_{周期}$ = 6 秒。

现在，使用示例B 6中的闪光器功率需求算出最大日负荷为：

E_{DL} = 34.0 瓦时/天 + 5.8 瓦时/天（闪光消耗）= 39.8 瓦时/天

G1067-1 TOTAL ELECTRICAL LOADS OF AtoN

1 INTRODUCTION

When planning to power an existing or new Marine Aids to Navigation (AtoN), it is highly advisable to choose the lowest consumption equipment to meet the operational requirements. Powered equipment to be considered with respect to consumption and efficiency include but are not limited to:

- light source and optic equipment;
- radio AtoN;
- sound signals;
- control and monitoring system.

2 HOW TO USE THIS GUIDELINE

This document is part of a set of guidelines and needs to be read in conjunction with the following documents (see Figure 2-1):

IALA Guideline 1067-0: Selection of Power Systems for AtoN and Associated Equipment.

IALA Guideline 1067-2: Power Sources.

IALA Guideline 1067-3: Electrical Energy Storage for AtoN.

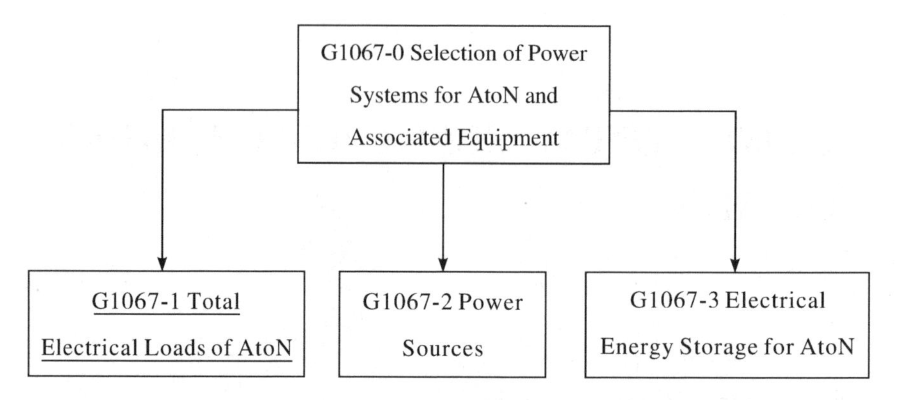

Figure 2-1 Overview of guideline structure

3 AtoN LOAD OVERVIEW

When determining the total electrical loads for a system, the following questions need to be answered.

- What needs power? —Identification of equipment and on which system.
- How much power? —Identification of the power consumption for each item in each mode of operation.
- How long is it needed? —Any character, duty cycle, during the periods of operations.
- When is it needed? —Daily, seasonal, weather dependent, traffic dependent and on-demand.

The first task in establishing the total electrical load is to estimate the length of time that each load will be operating. Estimating the length of time that a load is operating should be as accurate as possible, noting that, if the AtoN is operating only at night, the length of operating time will vary with the seasons.

A small error in estimating load operating time will be cumulative day after day, magnifying the error over the year. This could be critical for installations at high latitudes. If detailed information is not available, the "worst case" situation can be considered and the system designed for the longest winter night.

The design should ensure that switching devices turn the light on and off at the correct light levels to match the light-on periods calculated. At higher latitudes, there will be a marked seasonal effect on light-on periods.

It is advisable to consider the effect of a failure in one of the AtoN subsystems with regards to the power consumption of a complex AtoN system. Manufacturers should be encouraged to disclose the most probable failure modes and corresponding power consumption scenarios for supplied equipment.

3.1 QUIESCENT LOAD

The quiescent load is the power requirement of a piece of equipment which is idle, listening or monitoring. Transceivers generally have different load profiles when transmitting and when listening. Charge controllers typically consume more power during the day when the power electronics are energised, than at night or when the battery is fully charged.

3.2 DAY/NIGHT LOADS

Daytime or night time loads can vary significantly from season to season. As an example, a light operating at night at 58 degrees North latitude will be illuminated approximately 18 hours in December and less than 6 hours in June. These differences can have a significant impact on the size of the power source and the electrical energy storage system. Energy efficiency becomes very important in the higher latitudes. For example, 5 mA idle current for a lantern during daytime does not seem much, but for an autonomy period of 60 days about 7 Ah extra capacity is needed in the battery to allow for the idle current.

3.3 POWER DEMAND VARIATION

Power demand on AtoN sites is effected by numerous factors including but not limited to:

- temperature region;
- daytime/night time loads;
- latitude;
- weather conditions;
- equipment type and mode of operation;
- peak demand.

Temperature extremes and voltage fluctuations can also cause variation in the power requirements of loads. A resistive load will draw more energy as the voltage increases. Many components exhibit this characteristic.

Loads that operate during the daytime at photovoltaic powered aids to navigation will typically be exposed to higher system voltages as the array tries to recharge the battery. Components used should be able to handle these variations. The power consumption of the loads must be determined at the typical operating voltages.

In areas where there is often heavy cloud cover or fog the correct threshold setting of light switch-on and switch-off is important. If threshold for turn off is too high, it is possible that on a cloudy day the turn off of the light is delayed many hours from the intended time, which causes battery depletion.

Loads that operate both day and night may see different system voltages and thus average power consumption may need to be calculated to accurately predict system performance. Likewise, the power consumption of some loads varies as the temperature varies from ambient conditions.

The load demands at different latitudes will need to be adjusted to take into account the different night time periods; a major consideration at some latitudes must be the seasonal variation of load.

An accurate load profile from the vendor and an idea of the operating conditions are very helpful in estimating the actual power requirements; actual measurements at the AtoN location (or calculated) are vital to confirming the adequacy of the power system design.

As well as the above factors, careful design of the distribution infrastructure needs to be considered to ensure that aggregated instantaneous loads are met, without any impact on the equipment operation. This is becoming ever more critical for modern electronic and radio AtoN.

4 DAILY AND SEASONAL LOAD VARIATIONS

NOTE: This section is to be read in conjunction with IALA Guideline G1038: Methods and Ambient Light Levels for the Activation of AtoN Lights.

4.1 COMPUTATION OF A DAILY LOAD

The most important aspect of a primary or secondary battery powered system design is the calculation of the daily energy load (E_{DL}), for each item of

equipment. This is usually expressed as watt-hours per day (W·h/d).

$$E_{DL} = load \times duration\ of\ operation\ per\ day$$

Equation 1 Calculation of the daily load

Where:

E_{DL} is the daily energy load, measured in watt-hours (W·h).

Load is the power consumption of the equipment measured in watts (W).

Duration is duration of operation per day, measured in hours (h).

▶DUTY CYCLE

The above energy daily load calculation can be modified by the following formula, if the load is cycled.

$$\text{Duty cycle} = \frac{\text{Time ON}}{\text{Time ON} + \text{Time OFF}}$$

Equation 2 Duty cycle

4.2 SEASONAL VARIATION OF DAILY LOADS

Loads that are daylight controlled, that operate only during the day or only at night take more work to predict. Because the number of hours of daylight changes daily, the load will change daily. Most simple power system designs are based on the highest daily power consumption. In the Northern Hemisphere, this occurs around December 21 for night-time loads and June 21 for daytime loads. The dates are reversed for the Southern Hemisphere. A more precise method is to create a computer program, or use a computer spreadsheet, to calculate the load for each day of the year, and then assess energy balance during the most demanding period of operation.

Assuming that the loads switch on or off at sunrise or sunset, the first step in determining daily loads is to calculate the number of hours of daylight or, conversely, the number of hours of darkness. The number of hours of daylight in a day, $H_{daylight}$, is defined to be the number of hours between sunrise and sunset. The number of hours of darkness, $H_{darkness}$, is defined to be the number of hours between sunset and sunrise. The following equation can be used to calculate the number on hours of daylight. It should be noted that the equation is an approximations that is most accurate at the equator. The approximations has been adopted due to the fact that the Earth is an oblate spheroid and to account for the effects of refraction of the atmosphere. There are a number of alternative methods of calculating daylight hours available, these can be used but the results should be checked against the equations below or the results of measurement.

If all calculations are done in degrees then:

$$H_{daylight} = \frac{2}{15}\arccos\frac{-0.0151-\sin L * \sin D}{\cos L * \cos D}$$

Equation 3　Hours of daylight (degrees)

Where:

$H_{daylight}$ is the number of hours between sunrise and sunset.

L is the latitude of site, positive values for northern latitudes, and negative values for southern latitudes.

D is the sun's declination, positive values for northern declinations, negative values for southern declinations.

Note: The number −0.0151 is a number that has been derived to express the number hours of daylight that incorporates both the semi diameter and the refraction affects.

4.2.1　NOTE ON DECLINATION

The sun's declination ranges between 23.45° S (−23.45°) and 23.45° N (+23.45°). The day with the largest number of hours of darkness occurs on the date of the winter solstice. The declination on the date of the northern hemisphere's winter solstice is 23.45° S (−23.45°). The declination on the date of the southern hemisphere's winter solstice is 23.45° N (+23.45°).

To determine D for use in Equation 3, three different scenarios need to be considered depending on the Julian date to be used. The sun's declination (D) in degrees can be approximated as:

$D = 23.45 \sin [1.008 (n-80)]$　　for $n = 1-80$

$D = 23.45 \sin [0.965 (n-80)]$　　for $n = 81-266$

$D = -23.45 \sin [0.975 (n-266)]$　　for $n = 267-365$

Where n is the Julian date and all calculations are done in degrees.

4.2.2　NOTE ON HIGH LATITUDES

The above theoretical calculation is not mathematically possible for latitudes greater than 65.6° during certain periods of the year, whereby the following portion of the calculation must be replaced with the value of 1 or −1. So the following part of the $H_{daylight}$ equations

$$\frac{-0.0151 - \sin L \times \sin D}{\cos L \times \cos D}$$

will be less than −1 for a portion of the year and greater than +1 for a different

portion of the year. During these portions of the year for $H_{daylight}$ becomes as follows:

If $\frac{-0.0151-\sin L\times\sin D}{\cos L\times\cos D}<-1$, then $H_{daylight}=24$ (the sun does not set).

The number of hours between sunset and sunrise, $H_{darkness}$, can be readily calculated.

If $\frac{-0.0151-\sin L\times\sin D}{\cos L\times\cos D}>1$, then $H_{daylight}=0$ (the sun does not rise).

Using $H_{daylight}$:

$$H_{darkness}=24-H_{daylight}.$$

Equation 4 Hours of darkness

4. 2. 3 HOURS OF OPERATION

The hours of operation usually correspond to the hours of darkness ($H_{darkness}$), but extended operation hours occur due to National regulation for example. As such, a correction factors can be inserted easily. Modifiers to $H_{darkness}$.

This is a theoretical figure for when the Marine Aids to Navigation switched on and off. However, in practice, this is achieved with a photocell. The real figure could exceed this value, subject to climatic conditions, local conditions, shading and photocell adjustment. To account for these variations, particularly at high latitudes, a safety factor may be applied to the equation.

5 ACTUAL LOADS

5. 1 INCANDESCENT LIGHT SOURCES

NOTE: Under Light Sources, only lamps are discussed, LED are discussed in section 5. 2. The inclusion of other sources will need to be examined and if required calculation should be amended.

The most common load to all aids to navigation is the light. Lamps are classified by voltage, lamp current and power. Lamps that receive regulated output voltage from a flasher or voltage regulator consume the rated or calculated current. For example, a 12 volt, 100 watt incandescent lamp will consume 8. 33 amperes at rated voltage. This rating is only applicable to incandescent lamps in steady-state operation. Flashed lamps, while saving power during eclipse, draw more than the rated current during flash because of the cold current surge of the filament as shown in Figure 2-2.

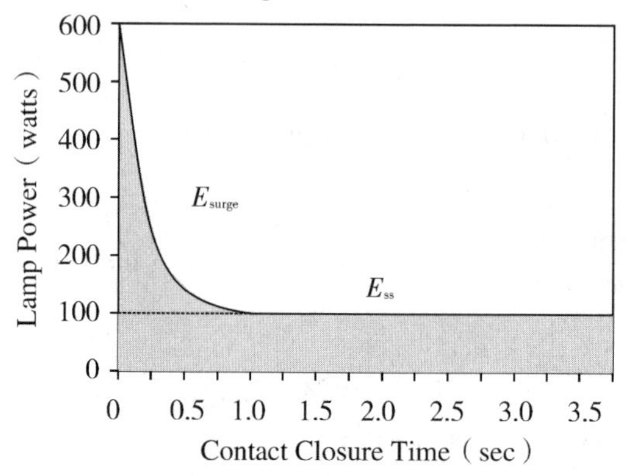

Figure 2-2 Typical power of a flashed lamp

The area under the curve represents energy (E). The energy consumed during one flash (E_1) can be divided into 2 parts:

$$E_1 = E_{surge} + E_{ss}$$

Equation 5 Total energy for one flash

Where:

E_1 is energy consumed during one flash.

E_{surge} is the portion of the consumed energy associated with the surge. This is represented by the upper area of the curve is in Figure 2-3.

E_{ss} is the energy associated with steady state power. This is represented by the rectangular area in Figure 2-3.

Consider E_{surge}: for any given lamp; E_{surge} can be considered a constant. A plot of the surge factor for common marine aids to navigation incandescent lamps in shown in Figure 2-3.

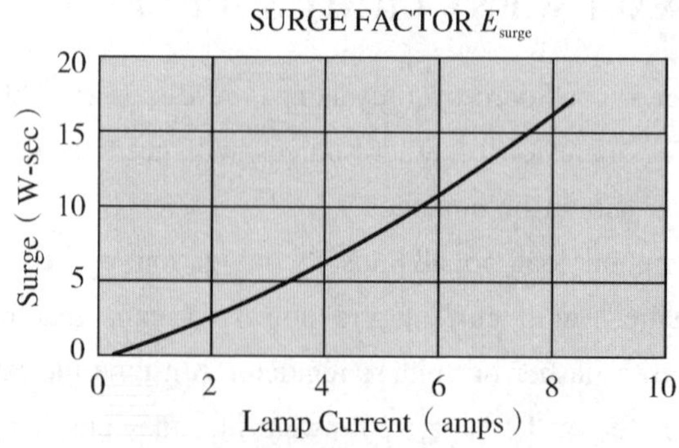

Figure 2-3 Surge Factor E_{surge}

E_{surge} can be approximated by the following equation:

$$E_{surge} = 0.1019 \times I^2 + 1.24 \times I - 0.3341$$

Equation 6 Approximation of E_{surge}

Where:

I is the lamp current in Amps.

E_{surge} is in watt-seconds.

Now consider E_{ss}:

$$E_{ss} = P_{ss} \times T_{flash}$$

Equation 7 Energy associated with steady state power

Where:

P_{ss} is the lamp's steady state power requirements (watts).

T_{flash} is the flash length(s).

E_{ss} is in watts-seconds.

To find the energy consumed in a day (daily load) multiply by the number of flashes in one day:

$$E_{DL} = E_1 \times \frac{H}{T_{period}}$$

Equation 8 Daily energy load from flash energy consumption

Where:

E_1 is the energy consumed per flash in watt-sec where $E_1 = E_{surge} + E_{ss}$.

H is the hours of operation of the light per day (hours).

T_{period} is the flash period (on plus off time) of the light (sec).

Note that E_{DL}, the daily load, conveniently comes out in W·h/d.

Combining Equation 6 and Equation 7 into Equation 8 we get:

$$E_{DL} = (E_{surge} + E_{ss}) \times \frac{H}{T_{period}}$$

Equation 9 Total daily energy from flashed lamp

The calculations listed above for lamp energy are approximations based on empirical data and may be used in lieu of actual measurements. Suppliers of lamps should be able to provide average lamp current values for all popular flasher rhythms. This data permits a simpler calculation for daily load.

NOTE: These surge effects decrease with the number of flashes in multiple flash characters.

5.2 LED LIGHT SOURCES

There are different principles of generating visual light and different levels of complexity of the circuitry used to drive a light emitting diode (LED). Some examples of these drive methods are:

- Passive power supply circuits;
- Active power supply circuits;
- Switching power supply circuits.

Powering LED based light sources may introduce issues requiring attention in the course of proper system integration at AtoN outstations. An example of this is the potential for any LED lantern to be a source of electromagnetic interference (EMI) and may in turn be susceptible to EMI from other equipment.

The power consumption of an array of LEDs or a single LED light source controlled by power input may be calculated similar to that of an incandescent lamp. LEDs however do not have the high starting current reflected in Figure 2-2 and for practical reasons E_{surge} becomes zero.

▶COMPLEX LED LIGHT SOURCES

Many contemporary complex LED light sources consist of several subsystems, integrating LED's, flashers, GPS receivers, measurement and monitoring modules within one product feeding from a single power. In such case, the power consumption budget of a product should be calculated based on manufacturer's information on all possible power modes expected to occur in the application scenario.

Most often the LED's are integrated in a lantern that houses an integrated LED power supply and a flasher, usually referred to as a self-contained lantern. The power consumption of such product can be divided into power consumption during flash, power consumption between flashes, and daytime quiescent power consumption.

$$E_{DL} = \left[P_{fl}(\mathrm{W}) \times \frac{T_{flash}}{T_{period}} + P_{bfl}(\mathrm{W}) \times \frac{1-T_{flash}}{T_{period}} \right] \times H_{darkness}\left(\frac{\mathrm{h}}{\mathrm{day}}\right) + P_{idle}(\mathrm{W}) \left[24 - H_{darkness}\left(\frac{\mathrm{h}}{\mathrm{day}}\right) \right]$$

Equation 10 Daily load for a complex LED light source

Where:

E_{DL} is the daily load in W·h per day.

P_{fl} is the power consumption during flash in Watts.

P_{bfl} is the power consumption between flashes in Watts.

P_{idle} is the daytime power consumption in Watts.

$H_{darkness}$ is the hours of darkness (or hours of operation per day).

To find the energy consumed in a day (daily load) some additional figures are needed:

T_{period} is the light's character period (sec).

T_{flash} is the total duration of flash in a period (sec).

5.3 METAL HALIDE

Metal halide discharge lamps are only ever used within rotating optic and require associated ballast to strike and maintain the ionised arc with the lamp. These ballast units can consume more than their lamp rating, so the ballast must be added when sizing a load. Again, manufacturers should be consulted to determine power requirements at the rated system voltage and temperature; and these values should be confirmed by measuring the devices in a realistic setting.

$$E_{DL} = P_{lb}\ (W) \times \textit{hours of operation per day}\ (h/day)$$

Equation 11 Daily load for a rotating optic

Where:

E_{DL} is the daily load in Wh per day.

P_{lb} is the measured/manufacturer figure for lamp and ballast power consumption in Watts.

5.4 FLASHER/CONTROL

The device used to flash or control the light source also requires power. Manufacturers of flashers/controls should be able to provide the power requirements of their units; an average value may be sufficient for high efficiency units. Otherwise, the demand during flash, eclipse and when idle (daytime) may be required to calculate the load profile. In general, the energy demand is calculated as a daily load, as follows:

$$E_{DL\,(average)} = P_q \times H_{daylight} + P_{bfl} \times (1 - \text{duty cycle}) \times H_{darkness} + P_{fl} \times \text{duty cycle} \times H_{darkness}$$

Equation 12 Daily load for a flasher

Where:

E_{DL} is the daily load in Wh per day.

P_q is the quiescent power consumption in Watts.

$H_{daylight}$ is the hours of daylight in hours per day.

P_{bfl} is the power consumption between flashes in Watts.

$H_{darkness}$ is the hours of darkness (or hours of operation per day).

P_{fl} is the power consumption during flash in Watts.

5.5 OPTIC ROTATION

Rotating optics have a load associated with the mechanism used to rotate the turntable assembly. Lighthouse services generally leave the turntable rotating continuously, both for operation at night, and during the day to prevent the sun from focusing through the lens panels and damaging the lamps or lamp changer. Therefore, the power requirements for the rotation mechanism and control system should be entered as a continuous load. This load may vary significantly with temperature, so be sure to identify the operating environment when requesting power demand information from the manufacturer.

$$E_{DL} = P_{motor}(W) \times \text{hours of operation per day}(h/d)$$

Equation 13 Daily load for a rotating optic

Where:

E_{DL} is the daily load in W·h per day.

P_{motor} is the motor and control system power consumption in Watts.

Rotating beacons may use Fixed-ON flashers to regulate voltage and operate the lamp changer; then the energy demand is:

$$E_{DL} = [P_{lamp}(W) \times H_{darkness}(h/d)] + E_{flasher}(W \cdot h/d) + E_{motor}(W \cdot h/d)$$

Equation 14 Daily load for a rotating optic and light source

5.6 SOUND SIGNAL

Sound signals operate over a wide voltage and temperature range. Request from the manufacturer of the signal the energy demand at the expected operating voltages and the expected operating temperatures.

$$E_{DL} = [P_{blast}(W) \times \text{duty cycle} + P_{silent}(W) \times (1 - \text{duty cycle})] \times \text{hours of operation/day}$$

Equation 15 Daily load for a sound signal

Where:

E_{DL} is the daily load in W·h per day.

P_{blast} is the sound signal and driver system power consumption during the blast, in Watts.

P_{silent} is the sound signal and driver system power consumption when silent, in Watts.

Duty cycle is the ratio between the on and total character period as a decimal value.

Sound signals under visibility detector control will require historic low visibility hour data to predict their operating time.

5.7 VISIBILITY DETECTOR

Visibility detectors can be used to minimise noise pollution from sound signals. These devices may use heaters in the projector and receiver windows to prevent condensation in cool weather. The temperature when these heaters turn on varies from model to model. You must determine the turn-on temperature of these heaters and have access to temperature data of the area. From this, an idea of how long the heaters will be activated (duty cycle) can be formulated. A data logging recorder is a useful tool to determine the duty cycle of the heaters, however failure to account for an unusually harsh cold spell may cause premature power system failure as the load will be substantially higher. The data logging recorder can also provide useful data as to how many hours the sound signal will be operating.

$$E_{DL} = P_{heater}(W) \times \text{duty cycle} \times 24\ h/d + P_{projector}(W) \times \text{duty cycle} \times 24\ h/d$$

Equation 16 Daily load for a visibility detector

Where:

E_{DL} is the daily load in W·h per day.

P_{heater} is the heater power consumption in Watts.

Duty cycle is the ratio between the on and total period as a decimal value.

$P_{projector}$ is the sensor head and control system power consumption per day.

5.8 CONTROL AND MONITORING SYSTEMS

5.8.1 CONTROL EQUIPMENT

Equipment used to control AtoN typically consume power. In general, the power consumption is rated for when the system is operating normally; i.e., main AtoN are operational and using the main power system. The loads associated with these devices are calculated as continuous loads.

$$E_{DL} = P_{active}(W) \times \text{hours of operation} + P_{standby}(W) \times \text{hours of operation}$$

Equation 17 Daily load for a monitoring system

Where:

E_{DL} is the daily load in W·h per day.

P_{active} is the power consumption of all of the active equipment when the AtoN is operational in Watts.

$P_{standby}$ is the power consumption of all of the standby equipment that is not operational per day in Watts.

5. 8. 2 MONITOR SYSTEMS

Monitor systems vary widely in complexity, means of transmission and power demand, with low energy models available for solar powered applications. Transmission methods will greatly affect the power demand. Phone lines, radios and satellite links each have different power requirements. They may use considerable power during data transfer. A strict regime should be established to control the time when the link is in operation. The power demand of the transmission device can usually be ignored if contact is made briefly once or twice a day. In this case, the quiescent demand is calculated as a continuous load and can be used to calculate the daily load. Many monitoring systems allow interrogation from the monitoring centre, and excessive operator-instigated requests for data from a single out-station can cause the energy drain to exceed the design parameters. Consult with the manufacturer of the unit to determine the actual power consumption for the application selected, but it is suggested to measure the current at the site to confirm the design data.

This therefore leads to a quiescent standing load and an increased communication mode when transmitting or receiving date based on a predicted duty cycle.

$$E_{DL} = P_{comms}(W) \times \text{duty cycle} \times 24\ \text{h/d} + P_{quiescent}(W) \times (1 - \text{duty cycle}) \times 24\ \text{h/d}$$

Equation 18 Daily load for a monitoring system

Where:

E_{DL} is the daily load in W·h per day.

P_{comms} is the power consumption during a typical data exchange in Watts.

Duty cycle is the ratio between the total communication time and a 24-hour period as a decimal value.

$P_{quiescent}$ is the quiescent standing power consumption per day.

Monitoring units may offer additional functionality like GPS signal reception and flashing synchronisation, measurement, etc. It is advisable to establish the mission specific power consumption profile of the product with consideration of all relevant factors like ambient temperatures, power supply voltages, and distance from shore stations, etc.

5.9 CHARGE CONTROLLER

Charge controllers are used to manage the energy and charge profiles from a source into a battery system. They provide overcharge protection, load disconnection in the event of low battery voltage and reverse current protection on photovoltaic systems. Charge controllers have both an efficiency and quiescent power requirements. The efficiency figure quoted by manufacturers is variable on power being converted by the regulator from the solar array. A typical figure being 98% efficient at full load. As this energy loss is not constant and varies with charge demand, this load is therefore captured as a factor (battery efficiency) within the IALA solar model, Methods and Ambient Light Levels for the Activation of AtoN Lights IALA Guideline 1039 Designing Solar Power Systems for Aids to Navigation (Solar Sizing Tool).

This then just leaves the quiescent load for the controller which can be considered a constant and is typically lower than 20 mA.

$$E_{DL} = P_{quiescent}(W) \times H_{operation}(h/d)$$

Equation 19 Daily load for a charge controller

Where:

E_{DL} is the daily load in W·h per day.

$P_{quiescent}$ is the quiescent standing power consumption per day.

$H_{operation}$ is the hours of operation per day.

5.10 AIS

5.10.1 GENERAL

AIS has the potential to replace or augment existing remote control and monitoring systems, as well as to provide AtoN service in its own right. Refers to IALA Recommendation A-126: The Use of Automatic Identification Systems (AIS) in Marine Aids to Navigation.

The power consumption of an AIS AtoN station depends on which type (Type 1, Type 2 or Type 3) of AtoN station is used, and on the setting of a number of parameters which may be configured in the unit. These parameters shown below are optimised to minimise power consumption.

- VDL access method: FATDMA will give substantially lower power drain than RATDMA.
- FATDMA slot selection: Channel A and Channel B slots should be close together in time, to minimise the period for which the processes in the AIS AtoN unit are active (Assuming the recommended Mode B is used).
- Reporting interval: An extended reporting interval will, of course, reduce power drain, but the interval should satisfy the guidance given in IALA Recommendation A-1261. ①
- The AIS AtoN unit should be designed or configured to enter into a "sleep" mode when not active.
- Number and types of messages transmitted;
- Transmitter power.

5.10.2 CALCULATION OF THE POWER REQUIREMENTS

The power requirement of an AIS AtoN unit transmitting Type 21 AtoN and Type 6 monitoring messages can be estimated by using the formula below:

► RATDMA Operation

$$E_{RX} = [P_s + (T_s + 60)(P_w - P_s)/T_r] \times 24 \text{ W·h/d}$$

Equation 20 Power requirement for RATDMA operation

Where:

E_{RX} is the power consumption when asleep or waiting to transmit.

P_s is the power taken by unit when asleep (Watt).

T_s is the time taken for unit to acquire slot map after waking up (secs).

P_w is the power taken by unit when awake, but not transmitting (Watt).

T_r is the reporting interval (secs).

$$E_{T21} = P_t \times \frac{4}{2250} \times \frac{60}{T_r} \times 24 \text{ W·h/d}$$

① Repeating of the AIS AtoN messages by a local AIS base station, during the reporting interval of the AIS AtoN station, may allow the reporting interval of the AIS AtoN unit to be extended. For example, the AIS AtoN may have a 10-minute reporting interval, but the local AIS base station repeats the AIS AtoN message every frame, i.e. every minute.

$$E_{T6} = P_t \times \frac{2}{2250} \times \frac{60}{T_m} \times 24 \text{ W·h/d}$$

$$E_{DL} = E_{RX} + E_{T21} + E_{T6} \text{ W·h/d}$$

Equation 21 Estimate of power consumption for an AIS unit transmitting Type 21 & Type 6 messages

Where:

E_{T21} is the power consumption for Type 21 message transmission.

P_t is the power taken by unit when transmitting (Watt).

T_r is the reporting interval (secs).

E_{T6} is the power consumption for Type 6 message transmission.

T_m is the reporting interval for monitoring message Type 6 (secs).

E_{DL} is the total daily power consumption.

5.10.3 FATDMA OPERATION

Use the same formulae as above, but the parameter T_s will be the time taken for the GPS receiver to obtain a position fix after waking up. (If a DGPS receiver is fitted T_s will be the time taken to obtain a DGPS corrected position fix after waking up.)

Note that P_w will be substantially lower when using FATDMA mode, as there is no requirement for a VHF receivers to be powered up.

5.11 RACON

The power consumption of RACONs is difficult to predict, as the load will be determined by the number of times the RACON is interrogated. Most RACONs have an upper limit on the number of responses broadcast if the unit is continuously interrogated due to a moored ship with the radar left on or an unusually busy channel. Consult with the manufacturer for high, medium and low power demand values for these devices and local pilots in the area to determine what level of traffic exists in the waterway. Alternately energy demand measurements can be made with an integrating ampere-hour or watt-hour meter over a 2-month period during maximum traffic to obtain a meaningful load profile.

$$E_{DL} = [P_t(\text{W}) \times \text{duty cycle} + P_q(\text{W}) \times (1 - \text{duty cycle})] \times 24 \text{ h/d}$$

Equation 22 Daily load for a RACON

Where:

E_{DL} is the daily load in W·h per day.

P_t is the power taken by unit when transmitting in Watt.

P_q is the power taken by unit between periods of transmission in Watt.

Duty cycle is the ratio between the total transmission time and a 24-hour period as a decimal value.

6 OTHER LOADS

6.1 NON-ESSENTIAL LOADS

Non-essential loads such as domestic lighting should ideally be under some form of automatic control to ensure that they cannot be left on and drain the power system. Such non-essential load should be sourced from an independent battery system to that of any AtoN and sized to meet the operational demands.

6.2 SEASONAL AIDS

Seasonal aids are operated for a portion of the year and either removed or secured during the period of non-operation.

It is advisable to ascertain that the equipment which is powered off for a significant period of time do not contain internal energy storage. Such energy storage is sometimes used to maintain power to memory devices backing up critical information that might become depleted during non-operation periods. In addition it is important that when powered up by remote control, such equipment does not create excessive power consumption once power is applied.

7 CONCLUSION

Once each load is fully characterised, then the sum of the loads for each day and each night must be calculated to determine the daily energy demand, and hence the system energy balance, battery daily minimum state of charge and seasonal minimum state of charge.

For designing of a solar system, these total loads can be used with the *Methods and Ambient Light Levels for the Activation of AtoN Lights* and IALA Guideline 1039 Designing Solar Power Systems for Aids to Navigation (Solar Sizing Tool) to develop an effective solar design.

Using E_{DL}, you can make a conservative system design with a couple of calculations. Calculation of E_{DL} for every day of the year using a design program and comparing it to the battery capacity or energy produced from a renewable energy source will allow you to design a less conservative but cheaper system.

The most critical success factors in the estimation of the energy requirements are:

- the definition of the total load;
- the definition of the load characteristics.

8 ACRONYMS

A·h	Ampere hour(s)
AIS	automatic identification system
AtoN	marine aid(s) to navigation
D	Suns declination angle
DGPS	differential global positioning system
°C	degrees centigrade
FATDMA	fixed-access time-division multiple access
GPS	global position system
h/d	hours per day
L	latitude
LED	light emitting diode
mA	milliampere
mW	milliwatt
n	number of the day in the Julian calendar
N	north
RACON	radar beacon
RATDMA	random access time division multiple access
s	second
S	south
V	Volt(s)
VDL	VHF data link
W	Watt(s)
W·h/d	Watt hours per day
W·s	Watt seconds

ANNEX A FURTHER EXPLANATION OF THE HOURS OF DAYLIGHT EQUATION

The derivation begins with the following basic astronomical equation which is stated without proof:

$$\cos\theta_h = \cos L \cos D \cos\omega + \sin L \sin D$$

Equation 23 The angle of incidence

Where:

θ_h is the incidence angle of the solar rays upon a horizontal surface = zenith distance = angle between solar rays and vertical line.

L is the latitude of site.

D is the solar declination.

ω is the hour angle.

(Note: All angles are in degree.)

From Equation 23:

$$\omega = \arccos\frac{\cos\theta_h - \sin L \times \sin D}{\cos L \times \cos D}$$

Equation 24 Hour angle

Sunrise is defined as the time at which the upper limb of the sun becomes visible. At sunrise the centre of the sun is 52 minutes of arc below the horizon as follows: the semi-diameter of the sun subtends an angle of 16 minutes of arc and the effect of atmospheric refraction accounts for an additional 36 minutes of arc. Therefore, sunrise will occur when, in Equation 24, $\theta_h = 90°52'$. Setting $\theta_h = 90°52'$ in Equation 24 allows for the calculation of $\omega_{sunrise}$:

$$\omega_{sunrise} = arccos\frac{\cos 90°52' - \sin L \times \sin D}{\cos L \times \cos D} = \arccos\frac{-0.0151 - \sin L \times \sin D}{\cos L \times \cos D}$$

Equation 25 Hour angle at sunrise

The amount of time between sunrise and local apparent noon is obtained by converting ω to time (15°of arc in longitude correspond to 1 hour):

$$H_{sunrise\text{-}noon} = \omega_{sunrise}/15°$$

Where:

$H_{sunrise\text{-}noon}$ is in hours.

The time from sunrise to sunset is double the time from sunrise to local

apparent noon:

$$H_{sunrise\text{-}sunset} = 2\ \omega_{sunrise}/15°$$

Equation 26 Time from sunrise to sunset-degrees

Combining Equation 25 and Equation 26:

$$= \frac{2}{15}\arccos\frac{-0.0151 - \sin L \times \sin D}{\cos L \times \cos D}$$

Equation 27 Time from sunrise to sunset

ANNEX B WORKED EXAMPLES

B 1 CALCULATION OF THE DAILY LOAD

For a continuous load of 1 Watt, for example, this calculation is expressed as (see Equation 1):

$$E_{DL} = 1\text{W} \times 24\ \text{h/d} = 24\ \text{W}\cdot\text{h/d}$$

This means that the energy source need to provide 24 watt-hours every day it operates.

B 2 CALCULATION OF DUTY CYCLE

Therefore, a cyclic daily load of 1 watt that operates 24 hours per day having a character of 3 seconds ON and 3 seconds OFF, is expressed as a daily load of (see Equation 2):

$$E_{DL} = 1\ \text{W} \times 24\ \text{h/d} \times \frac{3\ \text{sec ON}}{3\ \text{sec ON} + 3\ \text{sec OFF}} = 12\ \text{W}\cdot\text{h/d}$$

By cycling the load, the daily load in this case is half of a load operating at 100 percent duty cycle. This is an important aspect in conservation of energy.

B 3 CALCULATION OF HOURS OF DARKNESS

To find the maximum daily load for a cyclic load of 1 watt that operates at night, having a character of 3 seconds ON and 3 seconds OFF at 42 degrees N latitude, proceed as follows:

Since the load operates at night, the greatest daily load occurs at the time of the winter solstice when the sun's declination is −23.45°: $D = -23.45°$ perform all calculations in degrees (see Equation 3):

$$H_{daylight} = \frac{2}{15}\arccos\frac{-0.0151 - \sin(42) \times \sin D(-23.45°)}{\cos L(42) \times \cos(-23.45°)} = 9.1\ \text{h/d}$$

Giving:

$$H_{darkness} = 24 - H_{daylight} = 24 - 9.1 = 14.9\ h/d$$

Therefore, the maximum daily load (E_{DL}) is:

$$E_{DL} = 1\ W \times 14.9\ h/d \times \frac{3\ sec\ ON}{3\ sec\ ON + 3\ sec\ OFF} = 7.45\ W \cdot h/d$$

$D = 23.45\ \sin[1.008(n-80)]$ with $n = 45$ (Julian date for February 14 is 45)

To find the daily load for the same cyclic load on February 14 proceed as follows ($D = -13.54°$):

Perform all calculations in degrees:

$$H_{daylight} = \frac{2}{15} \arccos \frac{-0.0151 - \sin(42) \times \sin(-13.54°)}{\cos(42) \times \cos(-13.54°)} = 10.5\ h/d$$

Giving:

$$H_{darkness} = 24 - H_{daylight} = 24 - 10.5 = 13.5\ h/d$$

Therefore, the daily load is:

$$E_{DL} = 1\ W \times 13.5\ h/d \times \frac{3\ sec\ ON}{3\ sec\ ON + 3\ sec\ OFF} = 6.75\ W \cdot h/d$$

B 4 CALCULATION OF THE DAILY LOAD OF A FLASHED INCANDESCENT LAMP

What is the daily load of a 1.15 amp (13.8 watt) lamp that is flashing one second ON, one second OFF, on a day with 13.9 hours of darkness? Using Equation 9:

$$E_{DL} = (E_{surge} + E_{ss}) \times \frac{H_{darkness}}{T_{period}}$$

Calculating E_{surge} from Equation 6, where $I = 1.15$ amp

$$E_{surge} = 0.1019 \times I^2 + 1.24 \times I - 0.3341 = 0.1019 \times 1.15^2 + 1.24 \times 1.15 - 0.3341$$

$$E_{surge} = 1.2\ W \cdot s$$

Calculating E_{ss} from Equation 6 where $P_{ss} = 13.8$ W and $T_{flash} = 1$ sec

$$E_{ss} = 13.8 \times 1$$

Calculating E_{DL} from Equation 6 where $H_{darkness} = 13.9$ h/d and $T_{period} = 2$ sec

$$E_{DL} = (1.2 + 13.8) \times \frac{13.9\ h}{2\ sec} = 104\ W \cdot h/d$$

B 5 CALCULATION OF THE DAILY LOAD OF A FLASHED LED LANTERN

What is the daily load of a 2 W LED lantern that is flashing $\frac{1}{2}$ seconds ON,

$2\frac{1}{2}$ seconds OFF, on a day with 13.9 hours of darkness? The power consumption between flashes is 150 mW and the quiescent power consumption is 10 mW. Using Equation 10:

$$E_{DL} = \left[P_{fl} \times \frac{T_{flash}}{T_{period}} + P_{bfl} \times \left(1 - \frac{T_{flash}}{T_{period}}\right)\right] \times H_{darkness} + P_{idle}\ (24 - H_{darkness})$$

Where:

$P_{fl} = 2W$, $P_{bfl} = 0.15W$, $P_{idle} = 0.01W$, $H_{darkness} = 13.9h$, $T_{period} = 3s$, $T_{flash} = 0.5s$.

$$E_{DL} = \left[2 \times \frac{0.5}{3} + 0.15 \times \left(1 - \frac{0.5}{3}\right)\right] \times 13.9 + 0.01(24 - 13.9) = [0.333 + 0.125] \times 13.9 + 0.101 \approx 6.5\ W \cdot h/d$$

This example demonstrates that the power consumption between flashes can become a significant part of the total daily load in low power LED lanterns.

B 6 CALCULATION OF THE DAILY LOAD OF A LAMP FLASHER / CONTROL

An example showing a simple calculation for a control system using average power data see Equation 12:

$$E_{DL(average)} = P_{average} \times H_{operation}$$

Where:

$E_{DL(average)}$ is the average daily load in W·h per day.

$P_{average}$ is the average control system power in Watts = 240 mW continuous from the manufacturers data.

$H_{operation}$ is the number of hours of operation per day.

$$E_{DL} = 0.240 \times 24 = 5.8\ W \cdot h/d$$

By combining the energy demand of both the flashed lamp (example B 4) and the controller (see above) to obtain a total system energy demand we get the following:

$$E_{DL(total)} = 104 + 5.8 = 109.8\ W \cdot h/d$$

B 7 CALCULATION OF THE DAILY OPTIC ROTATION LOAD

As an example, a rotating beacon with a 2.03 Ampere 12 Volt lamp with a fixed rhythm flasher operating at night at 42 degrees N latitude with a 1.2 W continuous motor will have an energy demand of:

Using Equation 13:

$$E_{DL} = P_{lamp}(W) \times \text{hours of operation per day (h/d)}$$

Where:

E_{DL} is the daily load in W·h per day.

P_{motor} is the motor and control system power consumption in Watts.

$$E_{DL} = 1.2\ W^2 \times 24\ (h/d) = 28.8\ W \cdot h/d$$

Rotating beacons may use Fixed-ON flashers to regulate voltage and operate the lampchanger; then the energy demand is:

$$E_{DL} = [P_{lamp}(W) \times H_{darkness}(h/d)] + E_{flasher}(W \cdot h/d) + E_{motor}(W \cdot h/d)$$

Where:

E_{DL} is the daily load in W·h per day.

P_{lamp} is the lamp power consumption in Watts.

$H_{darkness}$ is the hours of darkness per day.

$E_{flasher}$ is the daily energy for the lamp flasher or control system in Watt hours per day.

E_{motor} is the daily energy for the optic motor and control system in Watt hours per day.

Given the following from above:

$P_{lamp} = 24.4$ W from above data.

$H_{darkness} = 14.9$ h/d from Calculation of Hours of darkness from example B 3.

$E_{flasher} = 5.8$ W·h/d from Calculation of the daily Load of a lamp flasher/control from example B 6

Assuming that the day and night power requirements are the same.

$$E_{DL} = (24.4 \times 14.9) + 5.8 + 28.8 = 398.16\ W \cdot h/d$$

B 8 CALCULATION OF THE AUDIBLE SIGNAL LOAD

For example, a sound signal with a power consumption of 21.6 watts during blast, and 0.24 watts when silent with a rhythm of one 3-second blast every 30 seconds, operating for 6 hours per day will have an energy demand of:

Using Equation 15:

$$E_{DL} = [P_{blast}(W) \times \text{duty cycle} + P_{silent}(W) \times (1 - \text{duty cycle})] \times \text{hours of operation/day}$$

Where:

E_{DL} is the daily load in W·h per day.

P_{blast} is the sound signal and driver system power consumption during the blast, in Watts.

P_{silent} is the sound signal and driver system power consumption when silent, in Watts.

Duty cycle is the ratio between the on and total character period as a decimal value

$$\text{Duty cycle} = \frac{3 \text{ sec ON}}{3 \text{ sec ON} + 27 \text{ sec OFF}} = 0.10 \text{ or } 10\%$$

$$E_{DL} = [21.6(\text{W}) \times 0.1 + 0.24(\text{W}) \times (1-0.1)] \times 6 = 14.256 \text{ W}\cdot\text{h/d}$$

B 9 CALCULATION OF A VISIBILITY DETECTOR LOAD

As an example, a visibility detector has a power demand of 6 watts with a heater load of 24 watts. The heaters turn on when the ambient temperature is below 10°C. Temperature data for the area indicates that the average minimum temperature is below 10°C between November and March and it is estimated that they will be activated 50% of the time during this period. The energy demands are:

Using Equation 16:

$$E_{DL} = P_{heater}(\text{W}) \times \text{duty cycle} \times 24 \text{ h/d} + P_{projector}(\text{W}) \times \text{duty cycle} \times 24 \text{ h/d}$$

Equation 28 Daily load for a visibility detector

Where:

E_{DL} is the daily load in W·h per day.

P_{heater} is the heater power consumption in Watts.

Duty cycle is the ratio between the on and total period as a decimal value.

$P_{projector}$ is the sensor head and control system power consumption per day.

$$E_{DL(\text{Nov.-Mar.})} = 24 \text{ W} \times 0.5 \times 24 \text{ h/d} + 6 \text{ W} \times 1.0 \times 24 \text{ h/d} = 432 \text{ W}\cdot\text{h/d}$$

$$E_{DL(\text{Apr.-Oct.})} = 6 \text{ W} \times 1.0 \times 24 \text{ h/d} = 144 \text{ W}\cdot\text{h/d}$$

B 10 CONTROL AND MONITORING SYSTEMS

For example, a typical 12 V telemetry systems has a quiescent current of 110 mA and monitors all of the input continuously. On change of state the unit will power up the modem and communicate to the monitoring centre. The communications typically last 3 minutes and the equipment current increases to 305 mA during this period. Typically the unit communicates 12 time a day.

From Equation 18:

$$E_{DL} = P_{comms}(\text{W}) \times \text{duty cycle} \times 24 \text{ h/d} + P_{quiescent}(\text{W}) \times (1-\text{duty cycle}) \times 24 \text{ h/d}$$

Equation 29 Daily load for a monitoring system

Where:

E_{DL} is the daily load in W·h per day.

P_{comms} is the power consumption during a typical data exchange in Watts.

Duty cycle is the ratio between the total communication time and a 24 hour period as a decimal value.

$P_{quiescent}$ is the quiescent standing power consumption per day.

$E_{DL} = P_{comms}(W) \times \text{duty cycle} \times 24\ h/d + P_{quiescent}(W) \times (1 - \text{duty cycle}) \times 24\ h/d$

$E_{DL} = 3.66(W) \times 0.025 \times 24\ h/d + 1.32(W) \times (1 - 0.025) \times 24\ h/d$

$E_{DL} = 2.196 + 30.88 = 33.084\ W \cdot h/d$

B 11 CALCULATION OF A CHARGE CONTROLLER LOAD

As an example, a small charge controller on a solar system has a peak efficiency at full load of 96% and a quiescent current of 10 mA on a 24 V system. The energy demand for this system is as follows:

Using Equation 19

$$E_{DL} = P_{quiescent}(W) \times H_{operation}(h/d)$$

Equation 30 Daily load for a charge controller

Where:

E_{DL} is the daily load in W·h per day.

$P_{quiescent}$ is the quiescent standing power consumption per day.

$H_{operation}$ is the hours of operation per day.

$$E_{DL} = 0.24(W) \times 24(h/d) = 0.576\ W \cdot h/d$$

B 12 CALCULATION OF AN AIS UNIT USING RATDMA ACCESS METHOD

As an example, an AIS unit fitted to a buoy has a sleep power demand of 12 mW, a wakes ups every 3 minutes during which the power demand is 0.6 W. The unit then takes 4 seconds to determine which slots to transmit in. The unit transmits on channel A and B during which the power for transmission is 30 W.

Using Equation 20:

$$E_{RX} = [P_s + (T_s + 60)(P_w - P_s)/T_r] \times 24\ W \cdot h/d$$

Equation 31 Power requirement for RATDMA operation

Where:

P_s is the power taken by unit when asleep (Watt).

T_s is the time taken for unit to acquire slot map after waking up (secs).

P_w is the power taken by unit when awake, but not transmitting (Watt).

T_r is the reporting interval (secs).

$$E_{RX} = \left[P_s + \frac{(T_s + 60)(P_w - P_s)}{T_m} \right] \times 24 \text{ W·h/d}$$

$$E_{RX} = [0.012 + (4 + 60)(0.6 - 0.012)/180] \times 24 \text{ W·h/d} = 5 \text{ W·h/d}$$

For message 21 the energy demand is:

$$E_{T21} = P_t \times \frac{4}{2250} \times \frac{60}{T_r} \times 24 \text{ W·h/d}$$

$$E_{T21} = 30 \times \frac{4}{2250} \times \frac{60}{180} \times 24 \text{ W·h/d} = 0.43 \text{ W·h/d}$$

For message 6 the energy demand is:

$$E_{T6} = P_t \times \frac{2}{2250} \times \frac{60}{T_m} \times 24 \text{ W·h/d}$$

$$E_{T6} = 30 \times \frac{2}{2250} \times \frac{60}{180} \times 24 \text{ W·h/d} = 0.213 \text{ W·h/d}$$

For the total daily load:

$$E_{DL} = E_{RX} + E_{T21} + E_{T6} \text{ W·h/d}$$

Equation 32 Estimate of power consumption for an AIS unit transmitting Type 21 & Type 6 messages

Where:

E_{DL} is the total daily power consumption.

E_{RX} is the power consumption when asleep or waiting to transmit.

E_{T21} is the power consumption for Type 21 message transmission.

E_{T6} is the power consumption for Type 6 message transmission.

$$E_{DL} = E_{RX} + E_{T21} + E_{T6} \text{ W·h/d} = 5 + 0.43 + 0.213 \text{ W·h/d} = 5.643 \text{ W·h/d}$$

B 13 CALCULATION OF A RACON LOAD

The calculation below is a typical example based on a single manufacture, due consideration must be given to the equipment manufacturers data in calculating the load.

For example, a RACON has a quiescent current of 24 mW when idle and 8.4 W when transmitting. The duty cycle is limited to 50%. Therefore, as a worst case scenario, if the RACON is continuously interrogated:

Using Equation 22:

$$E_{DL} = [P_t(\text{W}) \times \text{duty cycle} + P_q(\text{W}) \times (1 - \text{duty cycle})] \times 24 \text{ W·h/d}$$

Equation 33 Daily load for a RACON

Where:

E_{DL} is the daily load in W·h per day.

P_t is the power taken by unit when transmitting Watt.

P_q is the power taken by unit when between periods of transmission in Watt.

Duty cycle is the ratio between the total transmission time and a 24 hour period as a decimal value.

$$E_{DL} = [P_t(W) \times \text{duty cycle} + P_q(W) \times (1-\text{duty cycle})] \times 24\ \text{h/d}$$

$$E_{DL} = [8.4(W) \times 0.5 + 0.024(W) \times (1-0.5)] \times 24\ \text{h/d} = 101.1\ \text{W·h/d}$$

B 14 CALCULATION OF A SEASONAL ATON

To calculate the energy demand, a seasonal buoy operating at 42 degrees N with a 1.15 amp lamp with a FL6 (0.6) rhythm operating at night and deployed between April 1 and October 31 will have the following energy demand:

From section 4.2, calculate the suns declination (D) for the calendar limits:

$$D_{\text{Apr 1}} = 23.45 \sin[0.965(91-80)] = 4.320°$$

$$D_{\text{Oct 31}} = 23.45 \sin[0.95(308-266)] = 14.125°$$

Using Equation 3 and inserting the values of D from above and L for latitude to calculate the hours of daylight, and hence darkness.

$$H_{\text{daylight Apr 1}} = \frac{2}{15}\arccos\frac{-0.015-\sin 42° \times \sin 4.32°}{\cos 42° \times \cos 4.32°} = 12.7\ \text{h/d}$$

$$H_{\text{darkness Apr 1}} = 24\ \text{h/d} - 12.7\ \text{h/d} = 11.3\ \text{h/d}$$

$$H_{\text{daylight Oct 31}} = \frac{2}{15}\arccos\frac{-0.015-\sin 42° \times \sin 14.125°}{\cos 42° \times \cos 14.125°} = 10.4\ \text{h/d}$$

$$H_{\text{darkness Oct 31}} = 24\ \text{h/d} - 10.4\ \text{h/d} = 13.6\ \text{h/d}$$

Therefore, the night time load will be the greatest on October 31.

Then calculating the average energy demand using Equation 9:

$$E_{\text{lamp}} = (E_{\text{surge}} + P_{\text{ss}} \times T_{\text{flash}}) \times \frac{H}{T_{\text{period}}}$$

$$E_{\text{lamp}} = \left[1.2\text{W·s} + (13.8\text{W} \times 1\text{sec}) \times \frac{13.6\ \text{h/d}}{6\ \text{sec}}\right] = 34.0\ \text{W·h/d}$$

Where:

$E_{\text{surge}} = 1.2$ W·s, $P_{\text{ss}} = 13.8$ W, $T_{\text{flash}} = 1$ sec, $H = 13.6$ h/d, $T_{\text{period}} = 6$ sec.

Now determining the total maximum daily load using the flasher power demand from example B 6 is:

$E_{DL} = 34.0$ W·h/d + 5.8 W·h/d (flasher dissipation) = 39.8 W·h/d

第 G1067-2 号
电源

1　引言

1.1　范围和目的

本导则取代了 IALA 第 1044 号导则——用于航标的可再生能源（2005 年 6 月），同时纳入并取代 IALA 第 1042 号导则——用于航标的电源（2004 年 12 月）的文本。

本导则对电源的选择和设计提供了指导。本文件仅提供一般性建议，设备选择、操作和维护的具体信息由产品制造商提供。

本导则旨在帮助用户正确地选择和维护航标系统的电源。

1.2　能源系统选择的实践指导

IALA G1067-0 导则《航标及相关设备的电力系统选择》中的表 1-1 为选择不同类型和尺寸的负载所需的电力系统提供了初步的指示。

2　如何使用本导则

本文件是一套导则的一部分，需要结合以下文件（如图 3-1 所示）阅读。

IALA G1067-0 导则：航标及相关设备的电力系统选择；

IALA G1067-1 导则：航标的总用电负荷；

IALA G1067-3 导则：航标的电能存储。

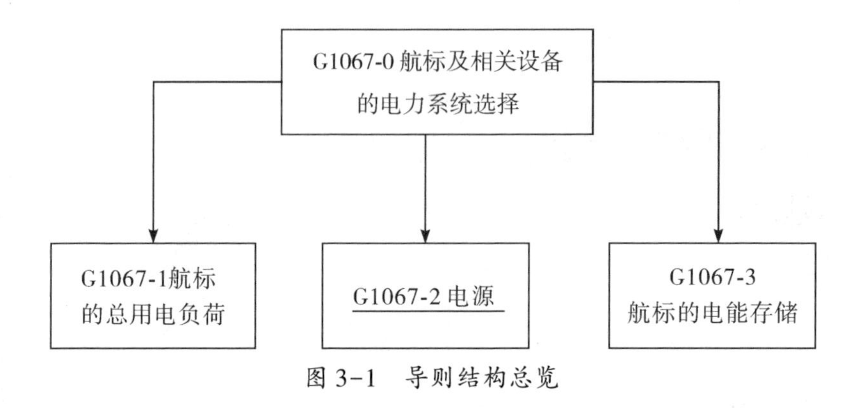

图 3-1　导则结构总览

3　交流市电

3.1　概述

首先应考虑现场或现场附近交流市电的可用性，可靠的交流市电应是首选能源。同时，可安装备用系统，防止停电时发生故障对航标可用性造成不利影响。

3.2　优点

- 不受系统负荷限制；
- 资金和运营成本低；
- 维护投入少。

3.3　缺点

- 依赖外部机构；
- 交流电源的供应可能不可靠；
- 远程维修时间延长；
- 可能需要一个定期维护的后备系统；
- 可能需要雷电保护和过电压保护系统；
- 自有电力线路维护需要成本；
- 需要进行定期测试和检查以确保安全；
- 维护人员承担的电气风险更高。

4 光伏发电

4.1 概述

如交流市电不可用、不可靠或成本过高，则太阳能应是首选方案。

在世界不同地区，光伏发电系统规模的确定方法可能不同。对于给定的负载或站点，没有唯一正确的设计解决方案。例如，对于给定的负载，可以增加光伏组件的面积、降低电池容量，反之亦然。

图 3-2　灯塔太阳能电池阵列

航标光伏发电系统最基础的部分是由光伏组件、充电调节器和蓄电池组成。光伏发电系统是一项成熟技术，许多供应商都能提供。如果设计得当并充分考虑海洋环境保护，那么光伏发电系统是非常可靠的，且为蓄电池充电使用最广泛的可再生能源。

一些国家已经出现了一种趋势，即缩短长射程视觉航标的射程，并结合现代高效光源，将航标转化为光伏能源。(如图 3-2 所示)

4.2 优点

- 能源可持续；
- 低技术维护；
- 使用寿命长；
- 技术成熟可靠；
- 运营成本非常低；
- 无能源购买成本；
- 提高了超低压系统的电气安全性。

4.3 缺点

- 性能受辐照度的影响较大，在没有日照的时期需要使用大量的存储能量；
- 环境影响（如沙、粉尘、鸟类排泄物、盐、遮阳等）会导致电量减少，这些问题可能增加维护成本；
- 需要较大尺寸以适应日照周期的变化；

- 容易受破坏或被盗；
- 为产生足够的电量，某些站点需要较大的安装面积；
- 在高纬度地区由于低辐照度，光伏投资可能没有效益；
- 易受风浪损害；
- 对历史灯塔的保护可能会限制光伏的使用；
- 在高温下性能下降。

5 风力发电

5.1 概述

风能是一种可再生能源，可以考虑用来为航标供电。风力发电机可作为混合动力系统的一部分作二次发电源。风力发电机有垂直轴和水平轴两种类型。(如图 3-3 所示)

图 3-3 挪威使用的各种风力涡轮机

5.2 优点

- 能源可持续；
- 备用二次电源；
- 电源昼夜可用；
- 小面积输出高能量；
- 无能源采购成本。

5.3 缺点

- 高维护要求；
- 不适合作为主要能源；
- 移动和旋转部件不够安全；

- 在特殊天气条件下易受损，如风湍流、冻雨、台风；
- 可能产生高噪声污染；
- 活动部件可能对鸟类造成伤害；
- 输出功率会因风力大小而改变；
- 暴风雨期间可能需要停止运作；
- 启动发电有最低风速要求；
- 支撑结构易被振动破坏；
- 风力涡轮机选址可能需要获得许可；
- 为了获得可靠的性能，需要层状气流。

6　波浪发电机

6.1　概述

波浪发电机（WAG）用于尾管浮标，可单独使用，也可作为混合系统的一部分使用，通常搭配太阳能使用。（如图 3-4 所示）

图 3-4　波浪发电机

6.2　优点

- 能量密度相对较高，通常在浮标上的输出功率为 6~100W；
- 电源全天可用，但受波浪状态影响；
- 是节省成本的可再生能源。

6.3　缺点

- 通常用于尾管浮标，可能不便于操作；
- 建设成本高；
- 高维护成本：通常需要每年对其进行维护；
- 可用性有限：单一能源；

- 噪声污染程度高；
- 海洋附着物会影响波浪发电机的性能。

7 燃料电池

7.1 概述

燃料电池技术是一项新兴的技术，且正在不断发展。在偏远地区，燃料电池可作为主要能源，也可以与光伏或风力发电机（混合系统）结合在航标上使用。

目前，市场上有两种与航标相关的燃料电池。

- 质子交换膜（PEM）电池：

PEM 使用气态氢作为直接燃料，适用于偏远地区的中大型固定灯器；

- 直接甲醇燃料电池（DMFC）：

该技术使用甲醇和水的混合物作为燃料。目前，该技术可以生产 100 瓦到 5 千瓦的电量。

7.2 优点

- 质子交换膜（PEM）单元内无活动部件；
- 低技术维护成本；
- 低污染物排放量；
- 低运营成本；
- 功率不受大多数天气情况影响。

7.3 缺点

- 燃料添加问题；
- 燃料安全和运输问题；
- 堆栈寿命有限；
- 部分类型燃料电池的低温性能差；
- 资金成本高。

8 柴油发电机

8.1 概述

柴油发电机一般用于偏远地区具有高功率要求的固定航标或作为市电

的备用设备。

应尽可能使用可再生能源系统代替柴油发电机。柴油发电可作为混合电力系统的备用部分，也可作为应急电源。在需要自主发电的地方，可能需要安装柴油发电机系统。(如图 3-5 所示)

图 3-5　法国柴油发电机安装实例

8.2　优点

- 良好的成本功率比；
- 技术成熟；
- 电力不受大多数天气情况影响。

8.3　缺点

- 安装复杂；
- 需要专用空间，即需要机舱；
- 需要定期维护；
- 产生噪声污染和大气污染；
- 需要定期加油；
- 燃料运输成本；
- 无人值守服务间隔较短，通常为 4~6 个月；
- 燃料储存环境风险处理必须因地而异。

9　汽油/燃气发电机

9.1　概述

一般来说，这些电力系统的使用方式与前一节中描述的柴油发电机系统类似。因其具有下面的缺点，不建议固定安装汽油发电机。

9.2 优点

- 部分优点参见8.2节；
- 良好的功率重量比。

9.3 缺点

- 部分缺点参见8.3节；
- 对燃料存放和运输安全有一定要求；
- 耐用性低于柴油发电机；
- 由于运行速度较高，会产生更多、更频繁的服务要求。

10 混合电力系统

10.1 概述

如果一种类型的能源系统（如光伏）不足以给电池充电，则可由所附加的另一种类型的能源系统为主电源进行补充，这被称为混合系统。(如图3-6所示)

图3-6 小型灯塔混合电力系统

混合电力系统的优点在于可以通过选择不同能源的方式更可靠地为航标系统供电。这可以通过组合不同的能源系统来实现，如光伏组件、风力发电机，甚至柴油发电机，以提供足够的供电能力为航标供电或给储能装置充电。

10.2 优点

- 可降低对储能系统容量的要求；
- 在供能方面较单一电源更为可靠。

10.3 缺点

- 系统更为复杂；
- 对维护的要求增加；
- 资金成本更高。

10.4 备注

操作人员应在拓展光伏发电机规模和增加二次能源之间进行成本比较。总的来说，备用电源通常不如太阳能光伏发电机可靠。

然而，对于大型光伏发电机（>1000 W），在夏季和冬季太阳辐射水平相差很大的纬度 40 度以上地区，可以考虑使用二次能源来降低系统电池容量，同时节省重量、设备体积和建筑空间。定期维护时可使用便携式发电机充电，从而将寿命周期成本降至最低。

10.5 设计注意事项

- 储能解决方案的选择；
- 能量存储空间必须能够容纳多个能源系统同时输出的峰值电流；
- 考虑技术组合。理想情况下，根据选择不同类型的混合电力系统，即被动式和机械式，选择理想的装置；
- 调节系统的选择；
- 应适当考虑调节器和输出并联连接的配制，即二极管保护。(见表 3-1)

表 3-1 电源组合可能性

项目	一次燃料电池	发电机	太阳	风	波浪	市电
二次燃料电池		0	++	++	+	++
发电机	0		++	++	0	++
太阳	++	++		++	++	+
风	++	++	++		0	+
波浪	+	0	++	0		0
市电	++	++	+	+	0	

注：++，首选；+，推荐；0，不推荐。

11 雷电/电涌保护

为了保护电力系统免受诸如雷击之类的破坏性电涌的影响，应考虑雷电保护。参见 2013 年 5 月的 IALA G1012 导则《关于保护灯塔等航标免受雷击损坏》。

12 安装

12.1 概述

应使用高横截面积（CSA）（mm^2）的电缆，以降低电阻并保证足够的机械强度。电缆应适应紫外线（UV）和海洋环境的影响。电镀（如镀锡铜线）可更好地保护导体。

在光伏系统中，一些制造商在组件背面安装防水接线盒。对于带有飞线的组件，应注意正确固定飞线，并确保飞线进入组件的位置不会对其施加过大的机械负荷。

12.2 公用电源

这通常由供电部门安排。如果最近的可用电源距离较远，那么供电部门可能会收取电缆路由到新位置的费用。这是非常重要的，应将其与其他电源供电的成本进行比较。

在所有情况下，供电部门将在最终连接之前检查安装情况。

12.3 光伏发电

12.3.1 概述

设计太阳能系统时，IALA G1039 导则《设计用于航标的太阳能系统》对 IALA 的太阳模式应用有所帮助，并提供一些信息。

太阳能安装装置的设计需根据特定使用的组件位置和类型而定。考虑到其工作环境，任何安装布置都应考虑在不同金属（框架/构件）之间使用绝缘体或支架进行适当的电偶腐蚀保护。

需要注意确保太阳能组件接线盒的水密完整性匹配组件的使用寿命，一般要求接线盒终身密封。

12.3.2 防止鸟类排泄物

在一些地区，鸟类排泄物会污染组件而引起安全问题。大量的驱鸟装置已经被设计出来，但没有一个装置是完全有效的。鸟刺（塑料或金属）是其中不错的选择，但效果也受不同地点的影响。垂直组件能减少此类问题，但也意味着需要加大尺寸。若选用金属鸟刺，则应考虑其可能对维护人员造成危害。

12.3.3　机械保护

对太阳能系统采取保护措施来减少海浪冲击、暴风雨、故意破坏、盗窃和浮标投放等所带来的损坏。将组件垂直安装在浮标上可降低组件的脆弱性，但会影响太阳能电池板的性能。

对于光伏系统，安装时应注意确保所安装的硬件不会对组件造成压力。此外，操作人员应注意组件在白天或任何季节时的全部或部分阴影，注意正在生长的草木和正在建设的建筑物，一个单元的阴影将导致串联系统中所有单元的电源输出出现部分或全部丢失的情况。

太阳能组件是贵重物品，需要使用合适的装置（特殊螺钉或螺母、焊接件等）以防止被盗。用告示牌表明其对海上安全的重要性可防止被盗。

组件后面的金属背衬和上方的透明前盖可保护组件不受破坏，但前盖会因传输速度较低而影响组件效率。如果前盖不能自动清洁，这种影响会更大。金属背衬可以保护背面有树脂的组件不被鸟啄。

12.3.4　组件倾斜角

对于固定的装置，太阳能电池阵列应尽可能面向赤道。组件与水平面之间的角度根据安装位置而变化。对于高纬度地区，组件阵列安装角度应该是纬度加上 20 度，以便在冬季最大限度地发电。对于低纬度地区，角度必须是纬度角，但为了尽量减少鸟类排泄物（即使有驱鸟措施）和污垢沉积的影响，最好不要有水平组件，倾斜角度不得小于 20 度。

浮标上的组件方向是随机的，组件通常分布在浮标的垂直轴周围，安装在一个陡峭甚至垂直的角度。这种安装方式可使雨水或海浪更为有效地自动冲洗盐或鸟类排泄物，也使上部结构的集成更容易、更有效地防止组件受损坏。这种安装角度的能量损失部分由水面反射补偿。一些部门的做法是将单个组件水平安装在浮标上的灯具上方。在南北半球的高纬度地区不建议水平安装组件。

12.4　风力发电

12.4.1　位置

所有的风力涡轮机在气流恒定且为层流的情况下性能最佳。但近海和沿岸的航标受附近建筑物或地形的影响，往往达不到这样的条件，其位置的选择通常为折中方案。

12.4.2　构件

安装风力涡轮机时，可能需要高成本的地面工程。如果安装在现有构件上，则需要合适的装配尺寸确保在各种天气条件下构件的耐受力和可维护性。安装过程通常采用拉线的方式来加固结构，但这需要合适的地面空间。

在设计和安装时应特别注意风力涡轮机的振动问题，尤其要注意避免风力涡轮机支架的固有频率。

12.4.3 安装

在选择更大输出功率的风力涡轮机（>1 kW）时，一个关键的考虑因素是现场的施工设备是否能将风力发电组件安装到位。

12.5 波浪发电机

这些小型装置通常安装在有尾管的浮标上。波浪发电机有效运行的一个关键因素是确保威尔斯涡轮机有良好的气流且波浪作用加压的空气回路能有效密封。

在设计和安装过程中，应充分考虑如何防止机组受波浪作用而损坏涡轮机。

安装时需要维护和清洁空气回路以确保设备有效运作，同时，清除会造成机组性能迅速降低的海洋附着物。

12.6 燃料电池

12.6.1 燃料管理

不同类型的燃料电池使用不同燃料，如氢、甲醇和丙烷等。所有这些都要求燃料得到保障和管理，既要适合于液体燃料的密封，又要适合于气体燃料的通风。这需要一个安全的稳固支撑悬放装置，但这将取决于在设备单元上的操作位置。即使在较小的甲醇机组上，燃料可存放在 25 升的小容器中，也可能需要安装用于装卸和加油的装置。

12.6.2 通风

燃料电池的放置位置既需要对环境有适当的保护，又需要足够的通风，以确保电池有效运行，因为该过程需要随时提供氧气来发电。

这个过程也会产生热量，热量可从通风系统释放到环境中，也可被燃料电池使用或为房间/建筑物提供背景加热。

12.6.3 水的处理

在发电过程中，副产品是纯水。这些水要么排放到环境中，要么被收集好以备日后使用。但操作人员需要采取适当的措施确保这些水不会冻结而妨碍装置的运行。

12.6.4 运行限制

根据所使用的燃料电池类型，启动时间是需要重点考虑的因素。一些燃

料电池需要在高运行温度（200～1000 ℃）下才能输出电能。这种“预热”阶段的能源要么来自燃料，要么来自外部电力。

12.7　柴油发电机

12.7.1　燃料管理

作为发电机安装的一部分，燃料库的大小要足以支持预期的运行需求。通常，其存储容量可从便携式发电机的 25 升到大型永久装置的 25000 升不等。这样的大型装置还具备远程监控可用剩余燃料的功能。

操作人员应注意燃料从燃料库到发动机的运输过程，确保将燃料泄漏的可能性降至最低以免污染环境。在设计和安装燃料发电系统的过程中应遵守地区、国家和国际的法规，并征求利益相关者的意见。

所有系统都具有燃料补充及采用可持续方案的需求。对于小型系统来说，这可能非常简单，但在较大的地点或离岸地区则需要使用更全面的解决方案，甚至考虑使用交付点。

如果发电机安装在室内，则需要提供设施来收集和保存任何泄漏到环境中的燃料。这些系统需要遵循地区、国家和国际的法规。

在简单燃料系统中，燃料依赖自身重力从油箱输送到发动机。在这种配置中，油箱和发动机顶部之间需有适当的高度差。如果无法确保这一点，那么即使燃油箱里燃油并没有用完，发动机也会停止。

12.7.2　通风

所有安装在室内的发动机都需要通风。所有便携式发电机均设计为在外部运行，并具有足够的通风以满足运行条件。任何通风都需要时刻提供足够的交换空气，为发电机在所有负荷和环境条件下提供稳定的运行环境。

通风可以是被动的（如通风口），也可以是主动的（如排风扇）。此外，通风口最好安装百叶窗，既可以在发动机不工作时隔离外部环境，也可以在发生火灾时阻断气流。百叶窗可以延迟开启，以使发动机温度上升到正常工作水平。

通风口总是成对安装的，一个是进气的（低位），一个是排气的（高位）。在理想情况下，进气口和出气口安装在房间的不同墙面上。这种安装方式不仅可以使室内的空气流动情况良好，而且能在通风机高风速的情况下保持通风。

12.7.3　废气管理

安装排气系统时，需要综合考虑许多方面：

- 柔性接头：分隔发动机振动与排气固定装置的重要部件；

- 隔热和降噪：减少内部和外部噪音，保护人员免受排气的高温影响；
- 排气罩：保护排气口，避免外部气流进入发动机。此外，如果排气口是水平的，为避免上浪水倒灌，应将其稍向下倾斜，以使任何进入排气系统的水自动排出；
- 材料：如果排气易受外部环境以及加热和冷却循环的影响，建议使用耐腐蚀材料，如 316 A4 不锈钢。

12.7.4 灭火剂

安装发电机时，应考虑防火要求及对生命和财产的保护。因此，在风险评估后需要安装自动消防系统，除非法规有其他要求。

12.7.5 装卸

所有安装的发电机重量都很大，需要提供适当的搬运设施，以便安装、维护和拆卸。

12.7.6 噪音与振动

发电机是一种非常可靠的电源，但它们都会产生大量的噪音。为了减少这些不良影响，可安装防震垫或将发电机安装在水平混凝土底座上，同时使用吸音材料。

13 维护

航标电力系统的维护应作为航标现场所有组件的总体维护计划的一部分进行规划。对维护需求的评估将影响初始投资，是生命周期成本的一部分。

对于电力系统，维护可能包括以下部分或全部：

- 检查所有电源部件是否有被腐蚀（尤其是电池间连接处和输出端）；
- 确认负荷需求在规定范围内；
- 检查电缆的连接状况。

13.1 公用电源

一般来说，公用设施供电系统所需的维护水平是最低的。较好的做法是对电缆和连接处进行一般的目视检查，同时检查所有保护装置和电缆绝缘的运行情况。在一些国家，这种测试是法律强制要求的。

13.2 光伏发电

在对大型太阳能电池板进行维护时，需要注意潜在的高电压和强电流。

安全维护的最佳方法是用适当大小的布罩覆盖电池板，同时在处理前留出时间让面板冷却。

对于光伏系统，检查封装材料是否有裂缝或变色，边缘是否分层，如冰晶效应。

应目视检查框架和固定件，确保无腐蚀或侵蚀。

应检查环境条件的变化，这可能影响光伏组件的阴影面积，如树木、新建筑物等。

可以通过使用标准太阳能电池在一个较长间隔周期中检查每个光伏板的性能（测试每块组件的最小短路电流和开路电压）。

13.3 风力发电

风力涡轮机的维护工作很大程度上受其运行地理位置的影响。因此，安装风力涡轮机对位置要求很高，在非层流气流区域或受海浪影响的区域，确保其持续运行的维护水平可能会更高。一般检查如下：

- 检查叶片和尾部是否存在开裂或其他损坏；
- 检查偏航（绕垂直轴旋转）操作是否平稳且无阻力；
- 目视检查支架和涡轮机上是否有腐蚀；
- 检查底座上的所有固定装置。

13.4 波浪发电机

为了有效地维护波浪发电机，需要一艘能够起吊尾管浮标的船舶。

维护波浪发电机的关键是确保尾管没有海洋生物附着。在操作空间有限的情况下，清除海洋附着物较为困难且需要花费很多时间。

如果在船只靠近时听不到波浪发电机工作的声音，则需要检查威尔斯涡轮机的状况。

13.5 燃料电池

除了补充燃料和处理收集到的水之外，燃料电池的定期维护次数是最少的。但是，如果燃料电池具有很高的运行要求，那么很可能需要让制造商更换燃料电池组。燃料电池组的一般使用寿命是4000小时，但在实际运行中使用寿命通常可达7000小时。

13.6 柴油发电机

因为柴油发电机由许多运动部件组成，所以维护要求相对较高。每年需要进行一系列检查，包括但不限于：

- 无论运行时间长短，更换机油和滤清器；
- 更换空气过滤器；
- 检查排气是否有烟灰，管道是否有泄漏；
- 在满载和轻载情况下，检查发电机是否完整运行；
- 目视检查发电机有无泄漏和连接处连接松动迹象，包括起动用蓄电池组的电解液和极柱腐蚀情况；
- 必要时检查冷却液位置；
- 检查并拧紧发电机输出的电气终端；
- 测量绕组绝缘电阻并记录数值。

13.7 巡检维护周期

巡检维护航标的周期通常由所安装的设备决定，可能是提前计划的维护、有条件的维护或者故障检修。有关三种方法的详细信息，请参阅第 1077 号导则《航标的维护》。

在许多地区，设计良好的系统每年巡检维护一次已经足够。但有一些地区则需要更频繁的维护，如工业扬尘、风沙或鸟类数量多的地区。在一些较热的气候环境下，最好每年维护两次，以便及时充满电池。

14 缩略语

AC	alternating current（交流电）
Amp	Ampere（安培）
AtoN	marine aid(s) to navigation（航海辅助标志，简称“航标”）
CSA	cross section area（横截面积）
DC	direct current（直流电）
DMFC	direct methanol fuel cell（直接甲醇燃烧电池）
kW	Kilowatt(s)（千瓦）
mm	millimetre（毫米）
PEM	proton exchange membrane（质子交换膜）
PV	photovoltaic（光伏）
UV	ultra violet (light)（10~380 nm）［紫外线（光）（10~380 nm）］
V	Volt(s)（伏特）
W	Watt（瓦）
WAG	wave activated generator(s)（波浪发电机）
℃	degrees centigrade（摄氏度）

G1067-2 POWER SOURCES

1 INTRODUCTION

1.1 SCOPE & PURPOSE

This guideline replaces IALA Guideline 1044 on Renewable Energy Sources for Aids to Navigation (June 2005) and includes text from IALA Guideline 1042 on Power Sources for Aids to Navigation (December 2004), which it also replaces.

This guideline provides guidance on the selection and design of power sources. While this document gives general recommendations, product manufacturers may provide specific instructions for selection, operation and maintenance of equipment.

This guideline is meant to assist users to properly select and maintain power sources used in Marine Aids to Navigation (AtoN) systems.

1.2 PRACTICAL GUIDE FOR THE SELECTION OF ENERGY SYSTEMS

Table 1-1 of IALA G1067-0: Selection of Power Systems for AtoN and Associated Equipment is intended to assist in the selection of power systems for required types and sizes of loads, however these are only approximate indications.

2 HOW TO USE THIS GUIDELINE

This document is part of a set of guidelines and needs to be read in conjunction with the following documents (see Figure 3-1):

IALA Guideline 1067-0: Selection of Power Systems for AtoN and Associated Equipment.

IALA Guideline 1067-1: Total Electric Loads of AtoN.

IALA Guideline 1067-3: Electrical Energy Storage for AtoN.

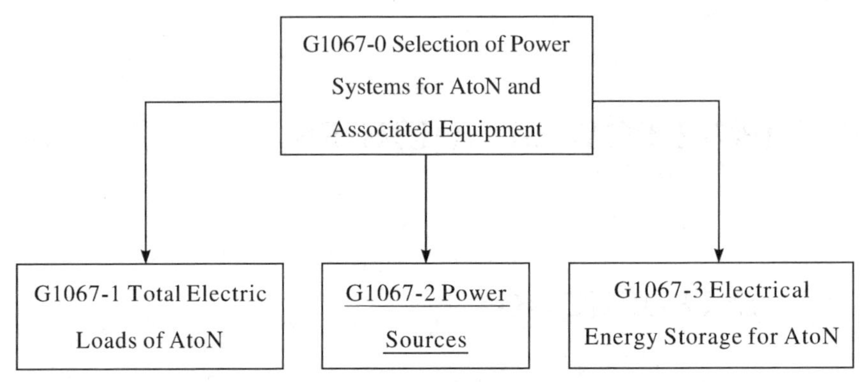

Figure 3-1 Overview of guideline structure

3 ALTERNATING CURRENT UTILITY POWER

3.1 GENERAL

The availability of alternating current (AC) utility power at or near the site should be the first consideration. Where a reliable AC power is available, it should be the preferred source of energy. Back-up systems may be installed in order to prevent AtoN failure in the case of a power outage to avoid adversely affecting the availability.

3.2 ADVANTAGES

- Load on the system is not critical.
- Low capital and running costs.
- Low maintenance.

3.3 DISADVANTAGES

- Reliance on external bodies.
- Possible unreliability of the AC power supply.
- Extended time to repair in remote locations.
- May require a back-up system that will need periodic maintenance.
- Lightning and overvoltage protection systems may be required.
- Maintenance cost of owned power lines.
- Periodic test and inspection required for safety.
- Higher electrical risk to maintenance staff.

4 PHOTOVOLTAIC POWER

4.1 GENERAL

If AC utility power is not available, reliable or too costly, solar power should be the preferred solution.

The approach taken in sizing the photovoltatic (PV) power systems may be different in different parts of the world. For a given load or site there is no one correct design solution. For example, for a given load, it is possible to increase the area of PV modules and decreasing battery capacity may be possible and vice versa.

Figure 3 - 2 Lighthouse solar array

An AtoN PV power system, in its simplest form, consists of a PV module, a charge regulator and a secondary battery. PV power systems are a well-proven technology and equipment is available from many suppliers. When properly designed with due consideration for protection from the marine environment, PV power systems are very reliable and are the most widely used renewable energy source for charging secondary batteries.

There has been a trend in some countries to reduce the range of long-range visual AtoN. This, combined with the use of modern high efficiency light sources, may mean that the AtoN can be converted to PV energy. (See Figure 3-2)

4.2 ADVANTAGES

- Sustainable source of energy.
- Low technical maintenance.
- Long life.
- Well proven and reliable technology.
- Very low operational costs.
- No energy purchase cost.
- Improved electrical safety on extra low voltage systems.

4.3 DISADVANTAGES

- Performance is subject to irradiance, and there is a need for large energy storage for period without sun.
- Deterioration of energy due to effects of the environment e. g. , sand, dust, bird fouling, salt, shading, etc. These issues may also increase maintenance costs.
- Need to oversize for variability in solar cycle.
- Susceptible to vandalism and theft.
- Large installation footprint required on some sites to generate sufficient energy.
- Cost of the systems may not be effective in high latitudes due to low irradiance.
- Susceptible to wind and wave damage.
- Heritage restriction may limit the use.
- Deterioration in performance at high temperatures.

5 WIND POWER

5.1 GENERAL

Wind energy is a renewable source of energy that can be considered in order to power AtoN. The wind generator can be used as a secondary source of power generation as part of a hybrid system. Wind generators are available in vertical and horizontal axis format. (See Figure 3-3)

Figure 3-3 Various wind turbines used in Norway

5.2 ADVANTAGES

- Sustainable source of energy.
- Alternate secondary source of power.
- Power available day and night time.
- High energy output from a small area.
- No energy purchase cost.

5.3 DISADVANTAGES

- High maintenance requirements.
- Not suitable as a primary source of energy.
- Moving and rotating parts (safety).
- Subject to damage under local weather conditions, e.g., wind turbulence, freezing rain, typhoon.
- Might produce high noise pollution.
- Moving parts can be dangerous to birds.
- Variable power production output.
- Might have to be stopped during storms.
- Minimum wind speed required to start power production.
- Can be destroyed by vibrations in the supporting structure.
- Permission may be required for siting of the wind turbine.
- For reliable performance laminar air flow is required.

6 WAVE ACTIVATED GENERATOR

6.1 GENERAL

Wave activated generators (WAGs) are used on tail-tube buoys. They can be used on their own or may be used as part of a hybrid system typically with solar power. (See Figure 3-4)

Figure 3-4 WAG

6.2 ADVANTAGES

- Relatively high energy density in floating AtoN with typically 60~100 W output power.
- Power is available night and day but is subject to wave state.
- Renewable energy source with associated cost savings.

6.3 DISADVANTAGES

- Normally used on a tail-tube buoys, which may be inconvenient to handle.
- High capital cost.
- High maintenance cost—typically installations need to be serviced at yearly intervals.
- Limited availability—single source.
- High level of noise pollution.
- Marine growths will impact on the WAG performance.

7 FUEL CELLS

7.1 GENERAL

Fuel cell technology is quite new and is under continuous development. The fuel cell can be used as primary energy source or in combination with PV or wind generator (Hybrid System) on AtoN in remote areas.

There are currently two types of fuel cells available on the market relevant to AtoN:

- Proton Exchange Membrane (PEM):

The PEM is using gaseous hydrogen as direct fuel and can be used on medium and major fixed lights in remote areas.

- Direct Methanol Fuel Cell (DMFC):

This technology is using a mixture of methanol and water as fuel. Currently, the technology can produce power from 100 W to 5 kW.

7.2 ADVANTAGES

- No moving parts in the Proton Exchange Membrane (PEM) cell.
- Low tech maintenance.
- Low pollutant emissions.
- Low operational costs.
- Power is independent of most weather conditions.

7.3 DISADVANTAGES

- Refuelling issues.
- Fuel safety and transportation issues.
- Stack lifetime is limited.
- Low temperature performance for some types.
- Capital cost.

8 DIESEL GENERATORS

8.1 GENERAL

Generally used for high power requirements on fixed AtoN at remote places or as back-up for utility electricity.

Renewable energy systems should be used in place of diesel generators wherever possible. Diesel generation may provide the reserve part of a hybrid system, or may be provided as an emergency power source. Installation of a diesel generator system may be considered necessary where domestic power is required. (See Figure 3-5)

Figure 3-5 Examples of diesel generator installation in France

8.2 ADVANTAGES

- Good cost to power ratio.
- Long established technology.
- Power is independent of most weather conditions.

8.3 DISADVANTAGES

- Complexity of installation.
- Dedicated space required, i. e. , engine room needed.
- Regular maintenance required.
- Produces noise and atmospheric pollution.
- Regular refuelling required.
- Cost of fuel transportation.
- Unattended service interval is short, typically 4~6 months.
- Fuel storage environmental risk has to be addressed at each site.

9 PETROL/GAS ENGINE GENERATORS

9.1 GENERAL

Generally, these power systems are used in a manner similar to the diesel generator systems described in the previous section. For the disadvantaged below, petrol engine generators are not recommended for fixed installations.

9.2 ADVANTAGES

- For the advantages, refer to section 8. 2.
- Good power to weight ratio.

9.3 DISADVANTAGES

- Refer to the section 8. 3.
- Fuel storage and transport safety implications.
- Less durable than diesel engine generators.
- Additional and more frequent service requirements due to the higher running speed.

10 HYBRID POWER SYSTEMS

10.1 GENERAL

If one type of system (e.g., PV) is not sufficient to recharge the batteries, then the addition of another type of power source can be used to supplement the main source. This is referred to as a hybrid system.

Figure 3-6 Small lighthouse hybrid power system

The advantages of a hybrid systems lies in the mix of power sources chosen to reliably supply an AtoN systems. This can be achieved by combining different sources of power, such as PV modules, wind generators, or even diesel generators to provide sufficient capacity to power the AtoN or recharge the energy storage devices. (See Figure 3-6)

10.2 ADVANTAGES

- Ability to reduce the capacity of the energy storage system.
- More reliable at providing power than a single source.

10.3 DISADVANTAGES

- More complex system.
- Increase in maintenance.
- Capital cost.

10.4 COMMENT

A cost comparison between oversizing a PV generator and adding a secondary energy source should be made, taking into account the fact that, generally, back-up sources are less reliable than solar PV generators.

However, with large PV generators (>1,000 W) and at latitudes above 40 degree where summer and winter solar irradiation levels are quite different, a secondary source can be considered for the purpose of reducing the system battery capacity, at the same time saving weight, equipment volume and building space. Portable generators have been used to minimise life cycle costs by including the recharge during scheduled maintenance.

10.5 DESIGN CONSIDERATIONS

- Selection of Energy Storage solution.
- Energy storage must be sized to accept the peak current output from multiple sources concurrently.
- Consideration to the mix of technologies. Ideally, select devices of different types, i. e. , passive and mechanical.
- Selection of a regulation system.
- Due consideration should be given to the mixing of regulators and the parallel connection of the outputs, i. e. , diode protection. (See Table 3-1)

Table 3-1 Power sources combination possibilities

Items	Primary fuel cell	Generator	Solar	Wind	Wave	Utility power
Secondary fuel cell		0	++	++	+	++
Generator	0		++	++	0	++
Solar	++	++		++	++	+
Wind	++	++	++		0	+
Wave	+	0	++	0		0
Utility power	++	++	+	+	0	

Key to the table: ++-Preferred +-Recommended 0-Not Recommended

11 LIGHTNING/SURGE PROTECTION

To protect a power system against destructive electrical surges such as lightning strikes, lightning protection should be considered. Refer to IALA Guideline 1012 on Protection of Lighthouses and AtoN against Damage from Lightning, May 2013.

12 INSTALLATION

12.1 GENERAL

Cables with a high cross section area (CSA) (mm^2) should be used to have a reduced resistance and a sufficient mechanical strength. Cables should be suitable for UV and the marine environment. The conductors would be better protected by plating, e. g., tinned copper wire.

In PV systems, some manufacturers supply their modules with waterproof junction boxes attached to the back. For modules with flying leads, care should be taken to properly secure the flying lead, and to ensure that no excessive mechanical load is placed on the lead at the point where it enters the module.

12.2 UTILITY POWER

This is usually arranged with the supply authority. Should the nearest available source be some distance away, then the supply authority may charge for routing a cable to a new location. This can be quite significant and should be compared against the cost of providing the power by some other source.

In all cases, inspection of the installation will be checked by the supply authority before final connections are made.

12.3 PHOTOVOLTAIC POWER

12.3.1 GENERAL

When designing a solar power system, Guideline 1039—Designing Solar Power Systems for Aids to Navigation will help with the use of the IALA solar model and will give some general information.

The design of any solar mounting arrangement will be specific to the location and type of modules used. Any mounting arrangement should consider suitable galvanic corrosion protection between dissimilar metals (frame/structure) using insulators or stand-offs, given the environment it is to operate in.

Care needs to be taken to ensure that the water integrity of the solar module junction box is suitable for the life of the module. This often required the junction box to be potted with for life.

12. 3. 2 PROTECTION FROM BIRD FOULING

In some areas birds cause real problems by fouling modules. A great number of devices have been designed but none are totally effective, and bird spikes (plastic or metal) are preferred. Devices working at some places don't work at others. Vertical modules reduce the problem, but in some cases, imply over sizing. The hazards presented to servicing personnel by metal bird spikes should be considered.

12. 3. 3 MECHANICAL PROTECTION

Protection to reduce the effect of wave impact, storms, vandalism, theft, and buoy-handling, is generally required. Vertical mounting of the modules on a floating AtoN reduces the vulnerability of the modules but affects the performance of the solar panel.

For PV systems, care should be taken at installation to ensure that the mounting hardware does not stress the module. Also, care should be taken with total or partial shadowing of the modules during the day or any season.

Attention should be paid to growing trees, grass and other structures. Note that shadowing of one cell in a module will cause the power output from all the cells in that series string to be partially or totally lost.

Solar modules are desirable items and as such, suitable devices (special screws or nuts, welded pieces, etc.) may need to be employed to dissuade thieves from removing equipment. Notice board indicating the importance of the installation for maritime safety may help in deterring loss.

Metal backing behind the modules, and a clear front cover over the modules might reduce the effect of vandalism, but generally a front cover affects the efficiency because of lower transmission. This effect will increase if the cover is not self-cleaning. Metal backing may protect modules that have resin on the back, from bird pecking.

12. 3. 4 TILT ANGLE OF THE MODULE

For fixed installations, the solar array should face the equator, where practicable. The modules are generally mounted so that the angle between the module and the horizontal plane varies depending on where you are on the earth. For high latitudes the array mounting angle should be latitude plus 20 degrees to maximise power generation during the winter months. For low latitudes the angle needs to be the latitude angle, but to minimise the effects of bird fouling (even with bird protection) and dirt deposits, it is better not to have horizontal modules and tilting should never be less than 20 degrees.

On floating AtoN, where the orientation of the modules is random, modules are usually distributed around the vertical axis of the buoy. Modules mounted at a steep angle, or even vertically, make automatic washing of salt or bird fouling by rain or sea spray more efficient. This can also make integration in the superstructure easier and protection from damage more effective. The loss of energy at such mounting angles is partially compensated by reflection from the water surface. Some authorities have a policy of mounting single modules horizontally above the lantern on buoys. The horizontal mounting of modules is not recommended for high latitudes in both the northern and southern hemispheres.

12.4 WIND POWER

12.4.1 LOCATION

All wind turbines perform best where the airflow is constant and laminar. This is often not available in the offshore and costal location of AtoN, either due to nearby structures or landscape. As such, any location is often a compromise.

12.4.2 STRUCTURES

When installing a wind turbine, the mounting structure may require significant ground excavation, which can be a significant cost. If mounting on an existing structure, the fabrication needs to be suitably sized to ensure survivability in all weather conditions and yet allow easy access for serviceability. Often guy wires are employed to rigidify structure, but this required the suitable ground space. Vibration is often an issue with wind turbine and care in the design and fitting of the mounting should take this into account, with particular care in avoiding natural frequencies of the mounting.

12.4.3 HANDLING

When selecting larger output wind turbine (>1 kW) a key consideration will be the site facilities available to handle the equipment into position.

12. 5 WAVE ACTIVATED GENERATOR

These small units are generally mounted on buoys which have tail tubes. A key factor to effective operation is ensuring that there is good airflow over the Wells turbine and that the air circuit that is pressurised by the wave action is effectively sealed.

Within the design and installation, consideration of how to baffle the unit from any wave action should be sufficient to ensure no damage to the turbine.

As part of the installation, a method of servicing and cleaning the air circuit is need to ensure good effective operation and the elimination of marine growth that can quickly reduce the unit's performance.

12. 6 FUEL CELLS

12. 6. 1 FUEL MANAGEMENT

The fuel used on the different types of fuel cells vary from hydrogen, methanol and propane to name but a few. All of these require the fuels to be secured and managed, with both suitable bunding for the liquid fuels and ventilation for the gaseous fuels. All will need a secure mounting, but this will be subject to the operational location on the unit. Mechanism may need to be put in place for handling and refuelling, although on smaller methanol units, the fuel can be provided in small 25 litre containers.

12. 6. 2 VENTILATION

The location where the fuel cell is to be sited needs to have both suitable protection from the environment but also sufficient ventilation to ensure effective operation, as the process requires a ready supply of oxygen to create electricity.

The process also produces heat, which can either be lost to the environment via ventilation or can be can be used within the fuel cell or provide background heating for the room/building.

12. 6. 3 MANAGEMENT OF WATER

In the process of producing the electrical power, pure water is produced as by-product. This either needs to be lost to the environment or needs to be captured for later disposal. Suitable measures need to be put in place to ensure this water does not freeze such that it impedes the operation of the unit.

12.6.4 OPERATIONAL CONSTRAINTS

Depending on the type of fuel cell used, consideration of the start-up time may be an important factor. Some fuel cell need to be brought up to a high operating temperature (200℃ to 1,000℃) before any electrical energy is available as an output. The source of energy for this "warm up" phase is either met from the fuel or can sometime be sourced from an external electrical power.

12.7 DIESEL GENERATORS

12.7.1 FUEL MANAGEMENT

As part of a generator installation, the size of the fuel store needs to be sufficient to support the anticipated operational demands. Typically, the stored volume can range from 25 litre for a portable generator to 25,000 litre for a large permanent installation. Such large installations also have means to remotely monitor the available volume.

Careful consideration of the transportation of the fuel from the fuel store to the engine, needs to ensure that likelihood of a leak is minimised to avoid environmental pollution. In the process of designing and installing a fuel system, there may be many local, national and international regulations that need to be followed and stakeholder to be consulted.

All systems will require the need for refuelling and a suitable solution should be implemented. For small system this may be very simple, but at larger or offshore location, a more comprehensive solution, taking into account the delivery point will need to be used.

Where a generator is fitted within a room, then facilities need to be provided to capture and hold any fuels spilts from escaping to the environment. Such systems needs to follow local, national and international regulations.

For simple fuel systems, the delivery of the fuel from the storage tank is driven by gravity. In this configuration, suitable difference in height between the storage and the top of the engine is required. Failure to ensure this is sufficient will result in the engine stopping when the fuel tank is only partially empty.

12.7.2 VENTILATION

Ventilation needs to be provided for all engines installed within building. All portable generators are design to operate externally and will have sufficient ventilation for the operating conditions. Any ventilation needs to provide sufficient air changes per hour to give a stable environment for the generator to operate in under all loads and environmental conditions.

The ventilation can be either passive, just a ventilator, or active, in the form of a vent fan. In addition, the ventilator will have a shutter fitted, both to keep the environment out when the engine is not operational, but also to shut off the airflow in the event of a fire. The opening of the shutter may be delayed to allow the engine temperature to rise to its normal operating level.

Ventilators are always fitted in pairs, an in (low down) and an out (high up), and ideally on different faces of the room. These locations will not only allow good cross flow of air in the room, but will allow the ventilation to operate even under high wind speeds on one ventilator.

12.7.3 EXHAUST MANAGEMENT

When installing an exhaust system there are a number of things that need to be integrated and considered. These are:

- Flexible joint: This is an essential component to isolate the vibration of the engine from the fixed installation of the exhaust.
- Lagging and silencing: Needed to both reduce the internal and external noise and protect personnel from the high temperatures of the surface of the exhaust.
- Exhaust cowling: Needs to be installed to protect the exhaust outlet from the environment getting into the engine. In addition, where the outlet is horizontal and subject to green water, a slight downward direction will allow any water that gets into the exhaust to be self-draining.
- Materials: Where the exhaust is subjected to the external environmental condition, along with the heating and cooling cycles, it is recommended that a corrosion resistant material is used, such as stainless steel 316 A4.

12.7.4 FIRE SUPPRESSANT

When installing a generator, consideration should be given to the protection of life and property as a result of a fire. As such, following a risk assessment or unless required by legislation, an automatic fire system may need to be fitted.

12.7.5 HANDLING

All installed generators are of a significant mass and suitable handling

facilities need to be provided to allow installation, maintenance and removal.

12.7.6 NOISE AND VIBRATION

Generators are an excellent reliability source of power, but they all produce significant amounts of noise and vibrations. To reduce this, anti-vibration matting or mountings on a level concrete base can be used along with noise absorbing materials.

13 MAINTENANCE

Maintenance of a power system at an AtoN should, of course, be planned as part of a total maintenance programme for all components of the AtoN site. Assessment of the maintenance required will be reflective of the initial investment and is part of life cycle costs. For the power system, maintenance will probably include some or all of the following:

- Inspect all power sources components for corrosion (especially at the inter-cell connections and at the output terminals).
- Confirm load demand is within specified limits.
- Check connections and condition of cables.

13.1 UTILITY POWER

As a general rule, the level of maintenance required on a utility powered system is minimal. It is good practice to do general visual inspections of cabling and connections, but also to check the operation of any protection devices and cable insulation. In some countries such tests are mandated by law.

13.2 PHOTOVOLTAIC POWER

When undertaking maintenance on large solar arrays, care needs to be taken due to the potentially high voltages and currents. The best method for safe maintenance is to cover the array with a suitable sheet, also allow time for the panel to cool before handling.

For PV systems, inspect for cracks or discoloration of the encapsulant, delamination in the borders, e.g., by ice effects.

A visual check should be made of the frame and fixing to ensure no corrosion or erosion.

A check should be made for changes in environmental conditions, which may result in shadowing of the PV modules, i. e. , trees, new buildings, etc. ; The performance of each PV panel may be checked at longer intervals by using a reference solar cell (to test at minimum the short circuit current and the open circuit voltage for each module).

13. 3 WIND POWER

The maintenance on a wind turbine will be significantly affected by the location where it is operational. In highly demanding locations where the airflow is not laminar or where they are subject to wave action, the level of maintenance may well be higher to ensure continued and continuous operation. Typical checks are as follows:

- Inspection of the blades and tail for cracking and damage.
- Check the yaw (rotation about the vertical axis) operation is smooth and resistance free.
- Visually inspect for corrosion on both the mount and turbine.
- Check all securing fixings on the mount.

13. 4 WAVE ACTIVATED GENERATOR

In order to effectively service a WAG, a vessel that is able to lift a buoy with a tail tube is required.

The key part to maintain a WAG is ensuring that the tail tube is clear of marine growth. This can take some time to clear and can be difficult to achieve, given the restricted access.

Should the WAG not be heard operating as the ship approaches, then checks on the condition of the Wells turbine will need to be done.

13. 5 FUEL CELLS

The periodic maintenance on a fuel cell is minimal, other than re-fuelling and disposal of any collected water. However, if the fuel cell has a high operational demand, then there may well be a requirement to change a unit to allow the fuel cell stack to be replaced by the manufacturer. A typical life of a stack being a guaranteed 4, 000 hours, but operationally 7, 000 hours is often achieved.

13.6 DIESEL GENERATORS

Because they are made of many moving parts, a generator has a relatively high maintenance requirement. On an annual basis a number of checks need to be done and these are detailed below, although this is not an exhaustive list:

- The oil and filter need to be changed regardless of low operational hours.
- Air filter change.
- Check exhaust is clear of soot and that the pipe has no leaks.
- Check the full operation of the generator, on both full and light load.
- Visual inspection of the generator for evidence of leaks and loose connections, including the starter batteries for electrolyte and post corrosion.
- Check coolant levels if require.
- Check and tighten the electrical terminations of the generator output.
- Measure the winding insulation resistance and record the values.

13.7 FREQUENCY OF MAINTENANCE VISITS

The frequency of visit to an AtoN are often dictated by the equipment fitted and will require either planned, conditioned or corrective maintenance. For more details on the three approached see Guideline 1077 Maintenance of Aids to Navigation.

In many locations, one maintenance visit per year should be adequate for a correctly designed system. There might be some sites where industrial fall-out, wind-carried sand, or a high bird population requires a more frequent schedule. In some hotter climates it may be better to visit twice per year for the timely topping up of the battery where applicable.

14 ACRONYMS

AC	alternating current
Amp	Ampere
AtoN	marine aid(s) to navigation
CSA	cross section area

DC	direct current
DMFC	direct methanol fuel cell
kW	kilowatt(s)
mm	millimeter
PEM	proton exchange membrane
PV	photovoltaic
UV	ultra violet (light) (10~380 nm)
V	Volt(s)
W	Watt
WAG	wave activated generator(s)
℃	degrees celsius

第 G1067-3 号
航标的电能存储

1 范围与目的

电力储存设备是电力系统的重要组成部分，要达到合适的应用标准，须进行合理的设计、安装、操作说明和维护。

本导则为常用于航标的储能设备提供了保养程序、作业条件和安全装卸等方面的指导。

本导则为一般性建议，制造商可能会提供针对具体设备的具体操作说明和维护指导。

本导则旨在帮助用户正确选择和维护用于航标的储能系统。

2 如何使用本导则

本文是导则的一部分，需要结合以下文件阅读（如图 4-1 所示）：

IALA G1067-0 导则：航标及相关设备的电力系统选择；

IALA G1067-1 导则：航标的总用电负荷；

IALA G1067-2 导则：电源。

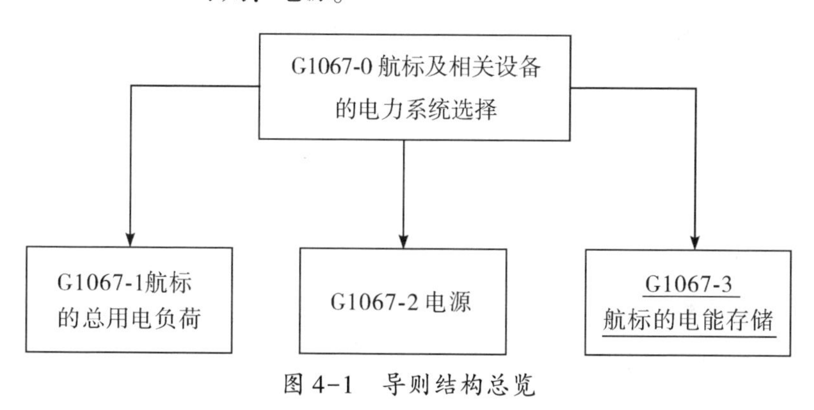

图 4-1　导则结构总览

3 电池储能类型

航标中使用的各种类型的电池储能系统分为一次电池（不可充电）和二次电池（可充电）。电池类型的选择一般在设计阶段进行，应满足当地环境及用户需求。下面的清单概述了常用的大多数电池类型，以及对应的优缺点。

注意：以下虽未列出全部电池类型，但是涵盖了航标应用中使用的主要类型。

3.1 一次（不可充电）电池

- 空气去极化干电池；
- 碳锌电池；
- 密封碱性电池；
- 锂电池。

3.2 二次（可充电）电池

二次电池的应用可分为两大类。

3.2.1 第一类

二次电池基本上作为主要电源使用，使用后可充电而不用丢弃。二次电池使用方便且节约成本（因为二次电池可以充电而无须更换），还可用于电量消耗超出一次电池容量的设备。

3.2.2 第二类

二次电池用作储能装置的应用，通常与电源连接并由电源充电。当电源不可用或不能满足负载要求时，二次电池能按需将储存的电量输送至负载。

- 铅酸电池：
  密封（免维护、阀控）电池；
  富液电解质电池（湿电池型）。
- 镍镉电池：
  开口式袖珍电池；
  开口式烧结电池；
  密封电池。
- 镍氢电池。

- 锂电池：
  锂离子电池；
  磷酸铁锂电池；
  锂聚合物电池。

4　各类航标电池的优缺点

4.1　一次电池类型

本节介绍了一次电池应用的电池设计说明。所有一次电池组均应考虑过电流保护。

4.1.1　空气去极化干电池

4.1.1.1　优点

- 输出功率高但会增加成本；
- 保质期长（2 年后容量仅降低 8%）。

4.1.1.2　缺点

- 有自呼吸要求；仅限安装于大部分岸基航标或通风良好的浮标。
- 需要适当的废弃处置。

4.1.2　锌碳电池

锌碳电池正被碱性电池所取代。

4.1.2.1　优点

- 是便宜可靠的密封类型电池，可用于不需要维护的独立导助航设备上，如浮标、信标和雷康（RACON），但在世界很多地区使用程度越来越低。

4.1.2.2　缺点

- 保质期短；
- 瞬时输出功率有限；
- 可用负载系数通常不超过 20%；
- 低温运行能力差。

4.1.3　密封碱性电池（如图 4-2 所示）

4.1.3.1　优点

- 生命周期比锌碳电池长；
- 在浮标灯和其他需要密封操作的设备上较为实用；

图 4-2　一次电池

- 低温性能好。

4.1.3.2 缺点

- 成本高，单位电压一般较低，这意味着要多组电池才可构成12 V系统。

4.1.4 锂电池

4.1.4.1 优点

- 重量轻，能量密度高；
- 保质期长。

4.1.4.2 缺点

- 如果操作不当，存在爆炸危险；
- 存在运输限制；
- 采购成本高。

4.2 二次电池类型

本节介绍了充电源可用情况下的充电电池。所有二次电池组均应考虑过电流保护。

4.2.1 富液式铅酸电池

4.2.1.1 优点

- 属于广泛应用的低成本电池，容易获取；
- 可批量供应，且尺寸、设计和容量多样；
- 良好的高放电率性能；
- 存放条件要求不高——可在干燥条件下储存；
- 电效率高；
- 电池电压高；
- 良好的浮充性能；
- 荷电指示状态明显（仅限湿电解质）；
- 技术成熟。

4.2.1.2 缺点

- 深度放电循环寿命相对较短；
- 能量密度低——通常为30~40 W·h/kg；
- 低温和高温性能差；
- 高自放电；
- 长期在放电条件下存放会导致电极硫化；
- 存在有害成分（腐蚀性电解质）；

- 需要足够的通风以避免爆炸；
- 危险且难以运输和安装；
- 低充电率可能会导致电池鼓包；
- 易出现临时故障。

4.2.2　阀控式铅酸电池

阀控式铅酸电池（VRLA）分为吸附式玻璃纤维网（AGM）电池和凝胶电解质电池。（如图 4–3 所示）

4.2.2.1　优点

- 免维护（无须加满）；
- 浮充寿命长；
- 良好的高放电率性能；
- 电效率高；
- 广泛应用的低成本电池，容易获取；
- 可批量供应，且尺寸、设计和容量多样；
- 技术成熟；
- 正常运行时无气体排放；
- 无泄漏风险；
- AGM 更适合寒冷气候。

图 4–3　发信台中安装的凝胶电池

4.2.2.2　缺点

- 长期在放电条件下储存会导致电极硫化；
- 能量密度相对较低；
- 存在有害成分（腐蚀性电解质）；
- 需要足够的通风以避免爆炸；
- 低温和高温性能差；
- 难以检查剩余电量；
- 深度放电可能导致电池故障；
- 需要过充电控制。

4.2.3　开口式（工业）镉镍电池（袖珍式）

4.2.3.1　优点

- 可靠、稳定；
- 循环寿命长（超过 2000 个周期，总寿命长达 25 年）；

- 自放电低；
- 可耐受深度放电；
- 可耐受高温和低温；
- 长期存放（任何电荷状态）；
- 充电率高。

4.2.3.2 缺点

- 需要足够的通风以避免爆炸；
- 能量密度低；
- 初始成本高于铅酸电池；
- 含有镉，以现有的回收设施，可能会增加回收处理成本；
- 未周期性地充放电会产生记忆效应（电压抑制）；
- 有运输危险。

4.2.4 开口式烧结镍镉电池

4.2.4.1 优点

- 放电曲线平稳；
- 能量密度较袖珍式高 50%；
- 优越的高放电和低温性能；
- 坚固、可靠，几乎不需要维护；
- 在任何电荷状态下及广泛温度范围内（-60~60 ℃）可长期存放；
- 自放电低；
- 循环寿命长；
- 预期寿命可超过 20 年。

4.2.4.2 缺点

- 需要足够的通风以避免爆炸；
- 含有镉，以现有的回收设施，可能会增加回收处理成本；
- 运输时存在危险；
- 能量密度低；
- 初始成本较高；
- 未周期性地充放电会产生记忆效应（电压抑制）；
- 需要过充电控制；

4.2.5 密封镍镉电池

4.2.5.1 优点

- 电池密封；

- 免维护运行；
- 循环寿命长；
- 预期寿命可超过 20 年；
- 良好的低温及高放电率性能；
- 任何充电状态下可长期存放；
- 快速充电能力；
- 可靠性强；
- 坚固，抗粗暴拆装。

4.2.5.2　缺点

- 需要充分通风，因为产生的氢气可能有爆炸的危险；
- 电池或充电设备设计不当时会导致热失控；
- 在某些特定应用中存在电压抑制；
- 由于电池含有镉（有害物质）而难以回收，依据现有的回收设施，这可能会增加处理成本；
- 成本高于密封铅酸电池；
- 运输困难。

4.2.6　镍氢电池

4.2.6.1　优点

- 免维护；
- 电池密封；
- 寿命长（预计 15 年）；
- 相对于体积和重量而言，能量密度较高；
- 正常运行时无气体排放；
- 循环寿命长（一般约 1200 个循环，但取决于放电深度）；
- 作业温度范围较大（一般为-20~60 ℃）。

4.2.6.2　缺点

- 成本高；
- 需要过充电控制；
- 存在热失控风险。

4.2.7　锂电池

4.2.7.1　优点

- 免维护；
- 电池密封；

- 长寿命（预计为 20~25 年）；
- 相对于体积和重量而言，能量密度非常高；
- 正常运行时无气体排放；
- 循环寿命长，但取决于充电方式；
- 低自放电；
- 充电效率高。

4.2.7.2　缺点

- 成本高；
- 电池所集成的电子管理系统复杂；
- 电池或充电设备设计不当时会导致热失控；
- 严格的运输限制；
- 必须以部分带电状态储存；
- 在 55℃以上的高温下会衰降；
- 充电温度低于-5℃时，会损坏电池；
- 存在爆炸和火灾危险。

4.2.8　锂聚合物电池

可选择锂聚合物电池，它具有与锂离子电池相似的特性，但更稳定。

4.2.9　锂离子电池

4.2.9.1　优点

- 免维护；
- 电池密封；
- 寿命长（预计为 20~25 年）；
- 相对于体积和重量而言，能量密度非常高；
- 循环寿命长，但取决于充电方式；
- 低自放电；
- 充电效率高；
- 与其他锂产品相比，固有安全性有所增强。

4.2.9.2　缺点

- 成本高；
- 严格的运输限制；
- 在 55 ℃以上的高温下会衰降。

5 二次电池的操作标准

本节详细说明了二次电池应用的操作标准。

这些电池系统可以向所连接的设备（负载）提供恒定、可变或间歇的电能，可以通过市电、可再生能源和混合系统充电。

5.1 计算所需容量

所需电池容量可通过以下方法确定：IALA 第 1067-1 导则《航标太阳能发电系统的总用电负荷》可用于确定航标太阳能发电系统所需电池容量；IALA 第 1039 号导则《航标太阳能发电系统设计》和 IALA 网站上的太阳能分选方案，可用于辅助计算。

5.2 电解液分层

电解液分层可能发生在富液式铅酸电池中。在这些电池中，可通过搅动电解液或定期增压充电来避免分层，在阀控式密封铅酸蓄电池中，可根据产品说明进行操作。

5.3 运输

电池通常在航标站点运行，往往难以抵达。任何选定的电池都应设计成能够承受正常运输和粗暴装卸过程中的机械应力。运输过程中必须使用合适的包装来保护电池。

一些电池可以在运输过程保持干爽，抵达现场后再按照厂家建议填充电解质并充电。

无论运输何种电池，均需要遵守一些限制或规定，如空运、陆运和海运的危险品限制要求等。

5.4 重量

为确保运输安全，重量是选择电池类型时的一个重要考虑因素。支撑结构的选择、设计和电池放置方式需要考虑电池重量以确保操作安全。

5.5 存储

厂家可提供安全储存的建议。

一些电池可能需要按照产品说明定期充电。

电池在存储过程中暴露在高温和潮湿环境中可能会导致容量下降。

5.6 作业温度

电池在使用过程中所面临的温度变化范围将显著影响电池寿命，这同时是电池选择的一个重要因素。电池应在其规定的温度下使用，若在这些规定的温度范围之外运行，将对电池的容量和预期寿命产生不利影响并可能造成危险。

5.7 物理保护

需要针对现场可能造成的不良后果提供物理防护：

- 温度梯度和极端温度；
- 阳光直射（紫外线辐射）；
- 扬尘或沙尘；
- 易爆性气体环境；
- 高湿度和洪水；
- 地震；
- 冲击、旋转、加速和振动（特别是在运输过程中和在轻型浮标上）；
- 严重的机械挤压或暴力拆解。

5.8 容量

储存容量单位是安时（A·h），并随使用条件（电解液温度、放电电流和终点电压）而变化。通常分别公布10小时（C_{10}）和5小时（C_5）的放电额定容量。由于100小时的数据通常用于光伏设备，因此还需要了解100小时（C_{100}）放电时间的容量。

5.9 循环寿命

循环寿命是指电池或电池组在指定条件下能反复充放电的循环次数。循环寿命通常指以固定放电深度（DOD）到充满电为一个循环通过电池下降到相关标准所规定的值（例如，通常为在25℃的额定温度下额定容量的80%）之前可以实现的循环次数来进行判定。

在光伏设备中，电池将暴露在大量的浅循环中并且电荷状态各不相同。因此，电池应该符合国际电工委员会的IEC 61427中关于光伏系统操作的模

拟所描述的测试要求。此外，制造商应标明电池容量降至相关标准规定值（如额定容量的 80%）前电池可达到的循环次数。

5.10　设计寿命

二次电池的设计寿命信息通常由制造商提供，并与航标站点的应用和可达性相匹配。在使用公用电源的情况下，二次电池的设计寿命成了整个系统的限制因素，因此，电池的设计寿命应在整个系统设计寿命背景下予以考虑。

5.11　充电参数

为了保持电池的最佳性能，必须恰当地控制电池的充电。控制方法具体取决于电池类型，此信息通常由制造商提供。不遵守充电参数进行操作将会缩短电池寿命并可能带来危险。过度充电不会增加电池中的电量，因此应避免过度充电，否则将会损坏电池。

为了延长电池寿命，应设置最大充电电压以确保电池在相当长的一段时间内充满电。这种调整代表了耗水过度和电池不完全充电之间的微妙平衡。

在安装铅酸电池前应根据厂家的建议进行预制（充电循环大约三次），以获得最大电池容量和使用寿命。

充电控制制度应考虑电池温度，特别是在高温和低温的应用情况下。用户应参考电池制造商的说明书以获取指引。

5.12　电池状态监测

根据风险情况，电池参数的监测和控制可能具有成本效益。根据位置的不同，可进行本地监控或远程监控。监控能对电池状况进行检查并在必要时采取补救措施，同时，也能预测电池可能存在的问题，并在这些问题导致故障之前采取措施。有关监测的一些详细信息，请参见 IALA 第 1008 号导则《航标遥测遥控》。

5.13　自放电

可再生能源设备中使用的电池的自放电必须非常低。自放电数值应由制造商说明并应符合相关电池标准的要求，用户需在设计系统时考虑这一点。

5.14　过放电保护

电池应防止过放电以避免容量的损失或损坏。当超过设计的最大放电深度时应减少负载或断开电路。根据制造商的详细说明，减载或断开机制也可用于防止过度放电引起的电池过早老化和出现故障。

5.15 浮标上的电池

浮标上的预期电池寿命可能比陆地站点的电池寿命短，这是电池极板的冲击负荷损坏造成的，对于富液式电池尤其如此。

为防止电解液溢出，浮标上通常使用吸附式玻璃纤维网（AGM）蓄电池和凝胶电解质电池，具体可咨询制造商。

5.16 性价比

还应注意的是，在某些地区可采用以较高电池更换频率换取较低电池价格的解决方案。这样的决策受到电池的供应、抵达航标站点的成本以及故障事件中快速到达的便利性等因素的影响。

6 储能系统的安全操作

电池是所有用于航标的储能系统的有机组成部分，因此，电池的安全操作是主要考虑因素之一。

6.1 电池安全问题

大型电池系统会产生极高短路电流。安装和维修电力系统中的任何部件时必须小心，防止短路。

某些类型的二次电池在充电过程中会产生氢气。电池充满电时会产生大量氢气，氢气很容易点燃并发生剧烈爆炸。应注意避免爆炸气体，并确保火源无论在电池正常运行时或故障时均处于受控状态。法规通常规定了特定电池类型的安全要求。制造商将协助提供相关电池的特定安全信息。

有些电池含有有害的化学溶液，可能对人员和环境有害。使用电池时，需要使用合适的个人防护设备和适当的工具以作为降低风险的有效方法。人员的培训和能力也是关键因素。

6.2 安装

除非干燥装运，否则电池应在收到后尽快安装。此外，电池应贮存在室内阴凉干燥的地方。所有二次电池应在安装后立即充电。

应最好将电池安装在清洁、干燥的区域，避免阳光直射（以防止单个电池发热以及紫外线照射）。外部电池盒应采用电绝缘材料制成，浅色，以防太阳加热，并在电池破裂时提供保护（仅限湿电池）。如果使用内部电池架，应使用绝缘托盘或隔层将电池与地面隔离，并妥善固定，以防倾倒。

按照产品说明安装电池互连。用无酸润滑脂涂抹电池柱和互连件，以防腐蚀。建议使用绝缘接头盖帽以防止意外短路，连接头盖帽应设计成有效且不妨碍日常维护任务的样式。

6.3 通风

铅酸电池和镍镉电池在充电时会产生氢气和氧气。有复合性能的二次电池只有在充气率超过复合率时才会充气。这通常发生在过充电期间。无复合功能的电池在充满电后会产生气体，并继续充电（浮动状态）。氢和氧的释放量并不取决于电池的类型和尺寸（铅酸电池或镍镉电池），而是取决于充电速度、电池数量和充电时间。电解液中的水会电解产生氢和氧。氢气浓度低于3%（按体积计）时是不可燃的，4%~8%的氢气暴露在明火或火花中会燃烧，8%以上的氢气会爆炸性燃烧。残余水分和不同金属之间的反应或溢出的电解质对金属的腐蚀也会在电池袋中产生氢气。

通风应根据 IEC 62485-2《二次电池和电池安装的安全要求》第二部分《固定电池》的要求，尽可能使用自然通风；如果自然通风不够，则可采用机械排气通风。

复合帽可用于各种类型的电池。使用复合帽将减少电池排放的氢气量，但仍需要电池室通风。电池制造商将提供电池所产气体量的详细信息。

6.4 回收与处置

国内和国际关于管理电池回收和处置的法律法规在不断发展。电池被认为是有害垃圾。如果处置不当，电池中的重金属会破坏环境；电池电解液具有腐蚀性，如果释放也会产生危害。虽然锂电池的污染风险很小，但由于其在未完全放电的情况下有可能发生爆炸性排气，因此，也必须将其作为有害垃圾进行处理。在大多数国家，铅酸电池和镍镉电池都是可回收的，尽管对镍镉回收的限制似乎随着相关成本的增加而增加。有关处置的进一步说明，请参阅 IALA 第 1036 号导则《航标中的环境管理》。

7 维护操作

7.1 一般注意事项

如果航标设备设计合理，电池可能只需最基本的维护。但最好是每年至少检查一次电池系统，或按照建议的时间间隔检查电池系统，以确保充电器、电池和辅助电子设备正常工作。

电池电源系统维护的基本要求可分为以下几组，可根据任何情况进行考虑和优化：

- 根据制造商要求进行电池维护；
- 应用和环境的要求，包括航标的类型、其预期操作模式、充电方法、环境；
- 用户/操作员的要求，包括安装地点的环境和对外开放性、维修人员的理念、技能和培训水平。

7.2 检查

进行检查时，建议采用规定流程，以确保电池保持良好状态。应记录所有检查的结果，包括测量值以及诸如主电源切断、放电测试、容量测试、存放时间和状态、顶部更新等。

充足的蓄电池记录是确定蓄电池状况的重要辅助手段。以下段落描述了检查程序的示例。

7.2.1 初始读数

初始读数是在电池投入使用时的读数。在系统无负载的状态下，电池充满电并闲置一段时间后，应读取并记录以下读数：

- 电池端电压和电池电压（如可能）；
- 电池电解质水平（如有）；
- 如有可能，将单个电池的比重读数校正为25 ℃；
- 环境温度；
- 充电器电压和电流限制。

记录这些初始读数以便将来比较是很重要的。

7.2.2 测量与记录

一般而言，在初始检查期间进行的所有测量应在安装期间继续进行。可以监测和记录以下附加测量值。

- 充电时，电池个体之间的温度应该是均匀的，并且温度差不得超过3 ℃；

- 先导电池（如使用）电压、比重和电解质温度（如有可能）；
- 使用去离子水。

7.2.3　电解质水平

对有些类型的电池需要定期补水以保持性能。务必遵守制造商关于电解质水平的要求。仅使用经批准的蒸馏水或去离子水再加注电池。电池不要加注过满。建议定期监测初始电解质水平，以确定再加注的频率。偏远地区可使用自动加注系统。

合理的耗水量是电池在正确条件下运行的最佳指示。若发现耗水量有任何显著变化，应立即进行调查。

耗水量过大可能表明充电电压过高或充电温度过高。当电池持续低电流或浮充状态时，耗水量可以忽略不计，这可能表示充电不足。

密封免维护电池不需要加水。压力阀用于密封，不破坏就不能打开。

7.2.4　目视检查

检查电池和电池区域（室、柜）的总体外观及清洁度。排除任何潜在污染，保持电池外壳、电池、通风口、端子和连接器清洁，因为灰尘和湿气会导致漏电。维护期间的任何溢出物都应用干净的布擦拭干净。可使用淡水或根据制造商的建议清洁电池。其他的目视检查包括：

- 检查电池盒是否有裂缝，以及电解液是否泄漏；
- 寻找连接处是否出现被腐蚀迹象；
- 连接处和端子螺钉应该涂上一层薄的无酸润滑脂防止腐蚀；
- 检查所有螺栓连接的紧密性（扭矩由制造商规定）；
- 检查是否有螺栓松动或连接不良，螺栓松动和连接不良可导致故障、高温甚至火灾；
- 检查通风系统状况，确认通风管道和过滤器正常工作，使通过电池室或电池柜的连续气流流通顺畅；
- 检查是否有漏电到地面的迹象；
- 检查电池支撑结构和外壳的完整性。

7.3　关于纠正措施的概述

以下是检查时应纠正的情况。

7.3.1　均衡充电

为了使电池达到统一的电压和比重水平，应按照产品说明进行均衡充电的纠正。发现以下任何情况时，都须进行均衡充电。

- 对于湿式铅酸电池，经温度和电解质水平校正后的单个电池的比重低于平均值 0.010 kg/L 以上，或者所有电池从检查时的平均安装值下降超过 0.010 kg/L；

• 充满电的电池电压为0.1 V，若超出制造商限定的额度，则停止充电电压。

如果这些情况持续很长时间，可能会导致电池寿命缩短。这不一定表示容量损失。

7.3.2 电池替换

发生故障的电池可以更换为具有相同品牌、类型、额定值、大致寿命和充电状态良好的电池。新电池不应与旧电池串联安装，除非别无他法。

7.3.3 电解质的分离

除非在充电过程中加以控制，否则大型电池中的电解质的分层会导致浓度变化，从而影响充电接受度、放电输出和寿命。控制分层的两种方法是：在过充期间以终装速率使板产生气体，或通过泵（通常是气升泵）搅拌电池电解质。

7.3.4 记忆效应

记忆效应描述了在重复的浅充/放电循环后导致镍镉烧结电池容量暂时降低的过程，通过一个由深放电和完全充电/过充组成的维护循环完全可逆。

8 缩略语

AGM	absorbed glass matt（吸附式玻璃纤维）
A·h	Ampere hour(s)（安小）
AtoN	marine aid(s) to navigation（航海辅助标志，简称“航标”）
Cx	capacity of a battery that has been completely discharged over a period of x hours（在 x 小时内完全放电的电池的容量）
DOD	depth of discharge（放电深度）
IEC	International Electrotechnical Commission（国际电工委员会）
kg	kilogram（千克）
kg/L	kilograms/litre（specific gravity）［千克/升（比重）］
PV	photovoltaic（光伏）
RACON	radar beacon（雷达信标，音译“雷康”）
UV	ultraviolet（紫外线）
V	Volt(s)（伏特）
VRLA	valve-regulated lead-acid（battery）［阀控铅酸（电池）］
W·h/kg	Watt hours/kilogram（瓦时/千克）
℃	degree(s) Celsius（摄氏度）

G1067-3 ELECTRICAL ENERGY STORAGE FOR AtoN

1 SCOPE AND PURPOSE

Electrical energy storage devices are an essential part of the power systems, and must be properly designed, installed, operated and maintained if they are to deliver the appropriate level of availability.

This guideline provides maintenance directives, operating criteria and safe handling guidance for energy storage devices commonly used in Marine Aids to Navigation (AtoN) applications.

While this document gives general recommendations, manufacturers may provide specific instructions for operation and maintenance of their specific equipment.

This guideline is meant to assist users to properly select and maintain energy storage systems used in Marine Aids to Navigation.

2 HOW TO USE THIS GUIDELINE

This document is part of a set of guidelines and needs to be read in conjunction with the following documents (See Figure 4-1):

IALA Guideline 1067-0: Selection of Power Systems for AtoN and Associated Equipment.

IALA Guideline 1067-1: Total Electric Loads of AtoN.

IALA Guideline 1067-2: Power Sources.

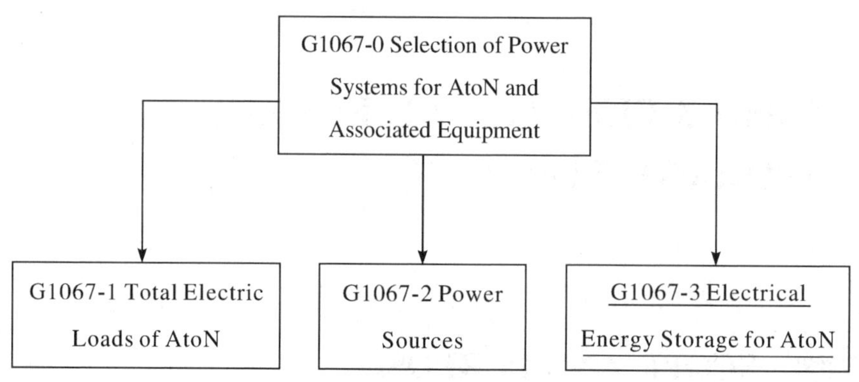

Figure 4-1 Overview of guideline structure

3 TYPES OF BATTERY ENERGY STORAGE

The various types of battery energy storage systems in AtoN services are primary batteries (non-rechargeable) and secondary (rechargeable) batteries. The choice of battery type will be made at the design stage and should be appropriate for use considering local constraints and needs of the user. The following listings outline the advantages and disadvantages of the majority of battery types in general use.

NOTE: The below is not an exhaustive list of battery types but covers the main types currently used in AtoN applications.

3.1 PRIMARY (NON-RECHARGEABLE) BATTERIES

- Air depolarised dry batteries.
- Zinc Carbon batteries.
- Sealed alkaline batteries.
- Lithium batteries.

3.2 SECONDARY (RECHARGEABLE) BATTERIES

The applications of the secondary batteries may fall into two main categories.

3.2.1 FIEST CATEGORY

Those applications in which the secondary battery is used or discharged essentially as a primary battery but recharged after use rather than being discarded. Secondary batteries are used in this manner for convenience, for cost

savings (as they can be recharged rather than replaced), or for applications requiring power drains beyond the capability of primary batteries.

3.2.2 SECOND CATEGORY

Those applications in which the secondary battery is used as an energy-storage device, generally being electrically connected to and charged by an energy source and delivering its stored energy to the load on demand when the energy source is not available, or is inadequate to handle the load requirement.

- Lead-acid batteries:
  sealed (maintenance-free, valve-regulated) batteries;
  flooded electrolyte batteries (wet battery type).
- Nickel-cadmium batteries:
  vented pocket-plate batteries;
  vented sintered-plate batteries;
  sealed batteries.
- Nickel-metal hydride batteries.
- Lithium batteries:
  Lithium-ion batteries;
  Lithium-iron-phosphate batteries;
  Lithium polymer batteries.

4 MAJOR ADVANTAGES AND DISADVANTAGES OF VARIOUS TYPES OF BATTERIES USED IN MARINE AtoN

4.1 PRIMARY BATTERY TYPES

This section covers the description of batteries designed especially for primary batteries use (primary energy source). It is important that over-current protection is considered on all primary battery banks.

4.1.1 AIR DEPOLARISED DRY BATTERIES

4.1.1.1 Advantages

- High output but increasing cost.
- Good shelf life (can be as little as 8% deterioration in 2 years).

4.1.1.2 Disadvantages

- Air breathing is required; limiting installations to mostly shore based

AtoN or buoys with carefully designed ventilation.

- Appropriate disposal is necessary.

4.1.2 ZINC CARBON

These are being superseded with alkaline types.

4.1.2.1 Advantages

- Cheap and reliable sealed types require no maintenance for stand-alone applications such as buoys, beacons and RACONs, but are increasingly unavailable in parts of the world.

4.1.2.2 Disadvantages

- Short shelf life.
- Limitation in instantaneous output power.
- Often not more than 20% load factor is available.
- Poor low temperature service capacity.

4.1.3 SEALED ALKALINE BATTERY (See Figure 4-2)

4.1.3.1 Advantages

- Longer life cycle to that of Zinc Carbon.
- Very useful in operating buoy lights and other applications requiring sealed secure operation.
- Good low temperature performance.

4.1.3.2 Disadvantages

- High cost, generally low voltage per unit meaning multiple sets of these batteries are needed to make 12 V systems.

Figure 4-2 Primary cells

4.1.4 LITHIUM

4.1.4.1 Advantages

- Low weight and high-energy density.
- Long shelf life.

4.1.4.2 Disadvantages

- There is an explosion risk if incorrectly operated.
- Transportation restrictions.
- High purchase cost.

4.2 SECONDARY BATTERY TYPES

This section covers the description of rechargeable batteries that are used where a charging source is available. It is important that over-current protection is considered on all secondary battery banks.

4.2.1 FLOODED LEAD-ACID BATTERIES

4.2.1.1 Advantages

- Popular low cost battery—readily available.
- Available in large quantities and in a variety of sizes, designs and capacities.
- Good high discharge rate performance.
- Reasonable storage life—can be stored in dry conditions.
- Electrically efficient.
- High cell voltage.
- Good float charge service.
- Easy state-of-charge indication (only wet electrolyte).
- Proven technology.

4.2.1.2 Disadvantages

- Relatively low deep discharge cycle life.
- Low specific energy—typically 30~40 W·h/kg.
- Poor low- and high-temperature performance.
- High self-discharge.
- Long-term storage in a discharged condition can lead to electrode sulphation.
- Hazardous contents (corrosive electrolyte).
- Need adequate ventilation to avoid explosive condition.
- Hazardous and difficult to transport and install.
- Stratification may occur with a low recharge rate.
- Rapid unexpected failure.

4.2.2 VALVE-REGULATED LEAD-ACID

Valve-regulated lead-acid (VRLA) batteries includes absorbed glass matt (AGM) and gel electrolyte. (See Figure 4-3)

Figure 4-3 Installation of gel batteries in a signalling float

4.2.2.1 Advantages

- Maintenance-free (no requirement for topping up).
- Long life on float service.
- Good high discharge rate performance.
- Electrically efficient.
- Popular low cost battery—readily available.
- Available in large quantities and in a variety of sizes, designs and capacities.
- Proven technology.
- No gas venting in normal operation.
- No spill risk.
- AGM is preferred for colder climates.

4.2.2.2 Disadvantages

- Long-term storage in a discharged condition can lead to electrode sulphation.
- Relatively low energy density.
- Hazardous contents (corrosive electrolyte).
- Need adequate ventilation to avoid explosive condition.
- Poor low- and high-temperature performance.
- Difficult to check capacity remaining.
- Deep discharge can lead to battery failure.
- Overcharge control required.

4.2.3 VENTED (INDUSTRIAL) NICKEL-CADMIUM BATTERIES (POCKET PLATE)

4.2.3.1 Advantages

- Reliable and robust.

- Long cycle life (more than 2,000 cycles, the total lifetime up to 25 years).
- Low self-discharge.
- Can tolerate deep discharge.
- Can tolerate high and low temperatures.
- Excellent long-term storage (in any state of charge).
- High recharge rate.

4. 2. 3. 2 Disadvantages

- Need adequate ventilation to avoid explosive condition.
- Low energy density.
- Higher initial cost than lead-acid batteries.
- Contains cadmium, which may increase cost of disposal depending on recycling facilities available.
- Memory effect (voltage depression) if not periodically deep cycled.
- Hazardous to transport.

4. 2. 4 VENTED-SINTERED-PLATE NICKEL-CADMIUM BATTERIES

4. 2. 4. 1 Advantages

- Flat discharge profile.
- 50% higher energy density than the pocket plate.
- Superior high-rate and low-temperature performance.
- Rugged, reliable, little maintenance required.
- Excellent long-term storage in any state of charge over a very broad temperature range (−60 ℃ to +60 ℃).
- Low self-discharge.
- High cycle life.
- Lifetime in excess of 20 years can be expected.

4. 2. 4. 2 Disadvantages

- Need adequate ventilation to avoid explosive condition.
- Contains cadmium, which may increase cost of disposal depending on recycling facilities available.
- Hazardous to transport.
- Low energy density.
- Higher initial cost.

- Memory effect (voltage depression) if not periodically deep cycled.
- Overcharge control required.

4.2.5 SEALED NICKEL-CADMIUM BATTERIES

4.2.5.1 Advantages

- Cells are sealed.
- Maintenance-free operation.
- High cycle life.
- Lifetime in excess of 20 years can be expected.
- Good low-temperature and high discharge rate performance capability.
- Long shelf life in any state of charge.
- Rapid recharge capability.
- Excellent reliability.
- Rugged, resist rough handling.

4.2.5.2 Disadvantages

- Needs adequate ventilation as hydrogen production can result in an explosion hazard.
- Thermal runaway in improperly designed batteries or charging equipment.
- Voltage depression in certain applications.
- Difficult to recycle as the battery contains cadmium (hazardous material), which may increase cost of disposal. Depending on recycling facilities available.
- Higher cost than sealed lead-acid battery.
- Difficult to transport.

4.2.6 NICKEL-METAL HYDRIDE BATTERIES

4.2.6.1 Advantages

- Maintenance free.
- Sealed battery.
- Long life (expected in order of 15 years).
- High energy density relative to volume and weight.
- No gas venting in normal operation.
- High cycle life (about 1,200 cycles is typical, but depends on the depth of discharge).
- Wide operational temperature range (−20 ℃ to +60 ℃ is typical).

4.2.6.2 Disadvantages

- High cost.
- Overcharge control required.
- Risk of thermal runaway.

4.2.7 LITHIUM-ION BATTERIES

4.2.7.1 Advantages

- Maintenance free.
- Sealed battery.
- Long life (expected in order of 20~25 years).
- Very high energy density relative to volume and weight.
- No gas venting in normal operation.
- High cycle life, but depends on the charging regime.
- Low self-discharge.
- High charging efficiency.

4.2.7.2 Disadvantages

- High cost.
- Complexity of battery integrated electronic management system.
- Thermal runaway in improperly designed batteries or charging equipment.
- Stringent transportation restrictions.
- Must be stored in a partial charged state.
- Degrades at high temperature above 55 ℃.
- Battery destruction if charged below −5 ℃.
- Hazard of explosion and fire.

4.2.8 LITHIUM POLYMER

Lithium-polymer batteries are available, and have similar characteristics to lithium-ion batteries but are more stable.

4.2.9 LITHIUM LRON PHOSPHATE

4.2.9.1 Advantages

- Maintenance free.
- Sealed battery.
- Long life (expected in order of 20~25 years).
- Very high energy density relative to volume and weight.
- High cycle life, but depends on the charging regime.

- Low self-discharge.
- High charging efficiency.
- Enhanced inherent safety compared to other lithium products.

4.2.9.2 Disadvantages

- High cost.
- Stringent transportation restrictions.
- Degrades at high temperature above 55 ℃.

5 OPERATIONAL CRITERIA FOR SECONDARY BATTERIES

This section specifies the operation criteria for secondary battery applications.

These battery systems can supply constant, variable or intermittent energy to the connected equipment (load) and can be charged by utility power, renewable energy sources and hybrid systems.

5.1 COMPUTING THE CAPACITY NEEDED

The required battery capacity can be determined by following guideline 1067-1 total electrical loads for aids to navigation for AtoN solar systems, IALA Guideline 1039—Designing Solar Power Systems for AtoN and the solar sizing program, found on the IALA website, can be used to aid the calculation.

5.2 ELECTROLYTE STRATIFICATION

Electrolyte stratification may occur in flooded lead-acid batteries. In these batteries, electrolyte stratification can be avoided by electrolyte agitation or periodic boost charging whilst in service and in VRLA batteries by operating them according to the manufacturer's instructions.

5.3 TRANSPORTATION

Batteries are often operated in AtoN sites, with challenging or limited access. Any selected batteries should be designed to withstand mechanical stresses during normal transportation and rough handling. Suitable packing to

protect the batteries must be used during transportation.

Some batteries may be transported dry and filled with electrolyte and charged in accordance with the manufacturer's recommendations on site.

When transporting any battery there may be restrictions or regulations that need to be complied with. Examples of these are dangerous goods by air, by road and marine transportation restrictions.

5.4 WEIGHT

Weight is an import consideration when selecting the type of battery to ensure suitable safe handling procedures are followed. Selection, design and placement of batteries in supporting structures need to consider the weight to ensure safe operation.

5.5 STORAGE

Manufacturers can provide recommendations for safe storage.

Some batteries may require periodic recharge in line with manufacturer's instruction.

A loss of capacity may result from exposure of a battery to high temperature and humidity during storage.

5.6 OPERATING TEMPERATURE

The temperature range during operation experienced by the battery will significantly affect battery life and is an important factor for the battery selection.

Batteries should be operated with the temperatures specified by the battery manufacturer. Operation of batteries outside these specified temperature ranges will have an adverse effect on the capacity and life expectancy and may prove hazardous.

5.7 PHYSICAL PROTECTION

Physical protection needs to be provided against consequences of adverse site conditions, for example, against effects of:

- temperature gradient and extremes of temperature;
- exposure to direct sun light (UV radiation);

- airborne dust or sand;
- explosive atmospheres;
- high humidity and flood water;
- earthquakes;
- shock, spin, acceleration and vibration (particularly during transport, and light buoy applications);
- severe mechanical abuse and rough handling.

5.8 CAPACITY

The storage capacity is expressed in ampere-hours (A·h) and varies with the conditions of use (electrolyte temperature, discharge current and final voltage). Normally the rated capacity for 10 hours (C_{10}) and 5 hours (C_5) discharge, respectively, is published. The knowledge of the capacity for a 100 hours (C_{100}) discharge time is also required as these times are commonly used in PV applications.

5.9 CYCLE LIFE

The cycle life is the number of cycles obtainable from a cell or battery under specified conditions.

The cycle life is normally given for cycles with a fixed depth of discharge (DOD) and with the battery fully charged in each cycle. Batteries are normally characterised by the number of cycles that can be achieved before the capacity has declined to the value specified in the relevant standards (e.g., 80 % of the rated capacity at a specified temperature, typically 25 ℃).

In photovoltaic applications the battery will be exposed to a large number of shallow cycles but at a varying state of charge. The batteries should therefore comply with the requirements of the test described in IEC 61427, which is a simulation of the PV system operation. The manufacturer should specify the number of cycles the batteries can achieve before the capacity has declined to the value specified in the relevant standards (e.g., 80 % of the rated capacity).

5.10 DESIGN LIFE

The design life is often supplied by the manufacturer and should be suitable

for the application and accessibility of the site. This is often a limiting factor when operated from a utility supply. The design life of the battery should be considered in the context of the overall system design life.

5.11 CHARGING PARAMETERS

To maintain optimum performance of a battery it is essential that its charge is properly controlled. The method of controlling is specific to the battery type and this information is usually provided by the manufacturer. Failure to follow this will shorten the life and could prove hazardous. Excessive overcharge does not increase the energy stored in the battery and should be avoided as it can result in damage to the battery.

For long battery life, the maximum charge voltage should be set to ensure the battery is fully charged for a significant period of time. This adjustment represents a delicate balance between excessive water consumption and the battery never becoming fully charged.

Lead acid batteries should be pre-formed (charge cycled approximately three times) prior to installation for maximum battery capacity and life in accordance with the manufacturers recommendations.

The charge control regime should take into account the battery temperature, particularly in high and low temperature applications. Users should refer to battery manufacturer specifications for guidance.

5.12 MONITORING OF BATTERY CONDITION

Monitoring and control of the battery parameters can be cost-effective, depending on risk. This can be locally or remotely, dependant on location. It allows battery condition to be checked, and remedial action taken as necessary. Monitoring will allow for the prediction of possible battery issues allowing action to be taken before these issues result in a failure. Some details on monitoring are available in IALA Guideline 1008—Remote Controland Monitoring of Aids to Navigation.

5.13 SELF-DISCHARGE

Self-discharge of a battery used in a renewable application must be very low. The self-discharge figure should be stated by the manufacturer and should meet the requirements of the relevant battery standard. This needs to be accounted for when designing the system.

5.14 OVER DISCHARGE PROTECTION

Batteries should be protected against over discharge to avoid capacity loss or damage. This can be achieved by load reduction or disconnect that operates when the design maximum depth of discharge is exceeded.

The use of a load reduction or disconnect mechanism, is also recommended to prevent premature ageing of the battery and possible failure, which may result from excessive battery discharge in accordance with the manufacturers details.

5.15 BATTERIES ON BUOYS

The expected battery life on buoys can be shorter than for a land station, due to shock-load damage of the plates especially for flooded batteries.

Absorbed glass matt (AGM) and gelled electrolyte batteries are often used on buoys to prevent spillage of electrolyte. Consult with the manufacturer.

5.16 QUALITY VERSUS PRICE

It should also be noted that in some areas an acceptable solution may be to use lower-priced batteries and accept that their replacement may be necessary more frequently than for specialist batteries. Such a decision will be influenced by the ability to source the battery, costs of accessing the AtoN site, and by the ease of fast access in the event of a failure.

6 SAFE HANDLING OF ENERGY STORAGE SYSTEMS

Batteries are an integral part of any energy storage system used in aids to navigation and safe handling is one of the key considerations.

6.1 BATTERY SAFETY ISSUES

Large battery systems are a source of extremely high short circuit currents.

Care must be exercised when installing and servicing any of the components in the power system to prevent shorting.

Some types of secondary batteries generate hydrogen gas during the charging process. Significant amounts of hydrogen gas are generated when the battery reaches full charge. Hydrogen gas ignites easily and produces an especially violent explosion. Care should be taken to avoid an explosive atmosphere and ensure all sources of ignition are controlled under both normal and fault operation. Often legislation dictates safety requirement for certain battery types. Manufacturers will help in providing the relevant battery specific safety information.

Some batteries contain hazardous chemical solutions that can be harmful to personnel and the environment.

When working with batteries, suitable personal protective equipment and appropriate tools need to be used as an effective way of minimising risk. Training and competency of personnel are also key issues.

6.2 INSTALLATION

Unless shipped dry, batteries should be installed as soon as possible after receipt. Otherwise, batteries should be stored indoors in a cool, dry area. All secondary batteries should receive a freshening charge immediately after installation.

Installation should preferably be in a clean, dry area and out of direct sunlight (to prevent individual cell heating and to protect against UV light). Exterior battery boxes should be constructed of an electrically insulating material, light coloured to prevent heating by the sun, and provide containment in the event of a cracked cell (wet batteries only). Interior battery racks, if used, should employ insulated trays or linings to isolate the cells from ground, and well secured to prevent tipping.

Install cell interconnections as per manufacturer's instructions. Coat cell posts and interconnections with acid-free grease to prevent corrosion. Insulated interconnection covers are recommended to prevent accidental short circuit, but in order to be effective they should be designed so as not to impede routine servicing tasks.

6.3 VENTILATION

Lead-acid and nickel-cadmium batteries produce hydrogen and oxygen gas when charging. Secondary batteries that employ recombination features will only gas when the gassing rate exceeds the recombination rate. This generally occurs during overcharge. Batteries without recombination features will gas when they are fully charged and continue to receive a charge (float condition). The amount of hydrogen and oxygen evolved is not dependent on the type and size of battery (lead-acid or nickel-cadmium), but rather on the charging rate, number of cells and the length of time charge is applied. Hydrogen and oxygen are produced as a result of electrolysis of the water in the electrolyte. Hydrogen concentrations of up to 3% (by volume) are non-flammable, at 4% ~ 8% hydrogen will burn if exposed to an open flame or spark, and above 8% hydrogen will ignite explosively. Hydrogen can also be produced in battery pockets by reaction between residual water and dissimilar metals or corrosion of metals by spilled electrolyte.

Ventilation shall be provided in accordance with IEC 62485-2 Safety requirements for secondary batteries and battery installations—Part 2: Stationary batteries, where possible natural ventilation should be used. If natural ventilation is unable to produce the necessary air changes, then mechanical exhaust ventilation can be employed.

Recombination caps are available for various battery types. These will reduce the amount of hydrogen vented by the battery but battery compartment ventilation will still be required. Details of volumes of gas produced will be available from the battery manufacturer.

6.4 RECYCLING AND DISPOSAL

The laws and regulations, both national and international governing the recycling and disposal of batteries are continually evolving. Batteries are considered hazardous waste. The heavy metals used in these batteries, when improperly disposed of, will damage the environment; the corrosive nature of battery electrolytes can also cause damage if released. While lithium batteries pose little pollution risk they must still be disposed of as hazardous waste because of their history of explosive venting if not fully discharged. Lead-acid and nickel-cadmium batteries are recyclable in most countries, although restrictions

on nickel-cadmium recycling appear to be increasing, along with the associated costs. For further guidance on disposal see IALA Guideline 1036—Environmental Management in Aids to Navigation.

 MAINTENANCE PRACTICES

7.1 GENERAL CONSIDERATIONS

In a correctly designed AtoN application, the battery may require minimal maintenance. However, it is good practice with a battery system to carry out an inspection of the battery system either at least once per year, or at the recommended interval to ensure that the charger, the battery, and the ancillary electronics are functioning correctly.

The basic requirements for the maintenance of a battery power system may fall into the following groups, which can be considered and optimised for any set of circumstances:

- Battery maintenance according to manufacturer's requirements.
- Requirements of the application and environment including the type of AtoN, its intended mode of operation, charging method, environments.
- Requirements of the user/operator including Installation site-environment and accessibility, maintenance philosophy, skill and training levels of maintenance staff.

7.2 INSPECTIONS

When an inspection is carried out, it is recommended that specific procedures should be adopted to ensure that the battery is maintained in a good state. The results of all inspections should be recorded, which can include the measured values as well as events such as mains power cuts, discharge tests, capacity tests, storage times and condition, topping updates etc.

Adequate battery records are invaluable aids in determining battery condition. An example of an inspection procedure is described in the following paragraphs.

7.2.1 INITIAL READINGS

The initial readings are those readings taken at the time the battery is placed in service. The following readings should be taken and recorded following a rest period on a fully charged battery with no load on the system:

- Battery terminal voltage and cell voltages if possible.
- Cell electrolyte levels, where accessible.
- Specific gravity reading of each cell corrected to 25 ℃, where accessible.
- Ambient temperature.
- Charger voltages and current limit.

It is important that these initial readings be recorded for future comparison.

7.2.2 MEASUREMENTS AND RECORDING

In general, all the measurements taken during the initial inspection should be continued for the life of the installation. The following additional measurements can be monitored and recorded.

- Cell temperatures whilst on charge should be uniform and the temperature differences between individual units should not exceed 3 ℃.
- Pilot-cell (if used) voltage, specific gravity, and electrolyte temperature (whenever possible).
- Use of de-ionised water.

7.2.3 ELECTROLYTE LEVEL

Some battery types require periodic filling of lost water to maintain performance. Always observe the manufacturers recommendation in relation to electrolyte levels. Use only approved distilled or deionised water to refill the cells. Do not overfill the cells. It is therefore recommended that initially electrolyte levels should be monitored regularly to determine the frequency of refilling. There are automatic refill systems available for remote locations.

A reasonable consumption of water is the best indication that a battery is being operated under the correct conditions. Any marked change in the rate of water consumption should be investigated immediately.

Excessive consumption of water may indicate being charged at too high a voltage or too high a temperature. Negligible consumption of water, with batteries on continuous low current or float charge, could indicate undercharging.

Sealed maintenance-free batteries do not require water refills. Pressure valves are used for sealing and cannot be opened without destruction.

7.2.4 VISUAL CHECKS

General appearance and cleanliness of the battery and battery area (room, cabinet). Exclude any potential contamination and keep the battery housing, cells, vents, terminals and connectors clean, as dust and damp cause current

leakage. Any spillage during maintenance should be wiped off with a clean cloth. The battery can be cleaned using fresh water or according to manufacturer's recommendation. Some additional visual checks can include:

- inspect for cracks and splits in battery cases or leakage of electrolyte;
- look for evidence of corrosion at the connections;
- the connections and terminal screws should be corrosion-protected by coating with thin layer of acid free grease;
- check tightness of all bolted connections (torque specified by manufacturer);
- loose bolts and bad connections can cause failure, high temperatures and even fire;
- condition of the ventilation system; verify that the ventilation ducts and filters operate correctly and allow continuous airflow throughout the battery room or cabinet;
- check for evidence of current leakage to ground;
- check integrity of battery support structure and enclosure.

7.3 OVERVIEW OF CORRECTIVE ACTIONS

The following items are conditions that should be corrected at the time of inspection.

7.3.1 EQUALISING CHARGE

The corrective action of an equalising charge to bring the cells to a uniform voltage and specific gravity levels, should be performed in accordance with the manufacturer's instructions. This is required whenever any of the following conditions are found.

- For wet lead acid cells, the specific gravity, corrected for temperature and electrolyte level, of an individual cell is more than 0.010 kg/L below the average or all the cells drop by more than 0.010 kg/L from the average installation value at the time of inspection.
- The fully charged cell voltage is 0.1 V outside of the manufacturer's recommended end-of-charge cell voltage. If these conditions are allowed to persist for extended periods, this can result in a reduction in battery life. This does not necessarily indicate a loss of capacity.

7.3.2 CELL REPLACEMENT

A faulty cell may be replaced by one in good condition of the same make, type, rating, approximate age and charged state. A new cell should not be installed in series with older cells except as a last resort.

7.3.3 STRATIFICATION OF THE ELECTROLYTE

The stratification of the electrolyte in large cells resulting in levels of varying concentration can limit charge acceptance, discharge output, and life unless controlled during the charge process. Two methods for stratification control are by deliberate gassing of the plates during overcharge at the finishing rate or by agitation of cell electrolyte by pumps (usually airlift pumps).

7.3.4 MEMORY EFFECT

The memory effect, describing a process which results in the temporary reduction of the capacity of a nickel-cadmium sintered cell following repetitive shallow charge/discharge cycles, is completely reversible by a maintenance cycle consisting of a thorough discharge followed by a full and complete charge/overcharge.

8 ACRONYMS

AGM	absorbed glass matt
A·h	Ampere hour(s)
AtoN	marine aid(s) to navigation
Cx	capacity of a battery that has been completely discharged over a period of x hours
DOD	depth of discharge
IEC	International Electrotechnical Commission
kg	kilogram
kg/L	kilograms/litre (specific gravity)
PV	photovoltaic
RACON	radar beacon
UV	ultraviolet
V	Volt(s)
VRLA	valve-regulated lead-acid (battery)
W·h/kg	Watt hours/kilogram
℃	degree(s) Celsius